ADVANCE PRAISE

"I found this book touching and authentic, as Kelli describes her personal journey of moving through fear, pain, and doubt to create a heart-led life. She takes us through her traveled and discovered steps so that we get to experience, with her, an arrival to her soul's calling. In reading her book, I felt enriched and once again found the deepest of gratitude for the many possibilities that exist. One of my favorite lines from the book: "That was not feeding her soul, it was appeasing her fear." Kelli's book shows us how to feed our soul."

STEPHANIE MERRIMAN, Merriman Management Support,
merrimanmanagementsupport.com

"In a time when so many of us unexpectedly struggle with the lives we find ourselves living, Kelli shows us we're not alone and there is a way through The Void to the other side. Using her own powerful journey, and those of her clients, Kelli thoughtfully and lovingly leads the reader through our own journey to reconnect and reacquaint ourselves to our unique destiny.

"Whether you're currently struggling to reconnect to your purpose or you just want some simple, yet powerful, tools for dealing with temporary changes, *The Destiny Roadmap* is a rich, daily practice to help you clear away the confusion and find clarity to confidently move forward."

KRIS PLACHY, Leadership Coach, sheisrelentless.com

"If you are truly ready to stop avoiding, put the excuses behind you, and get s*** done, then use (and I mean use, not just read!) *The Destiny Roadmap*. Kelli Reese imparts great life lessons with practical steps to help pull you into the present moment, and get you into trust and action mode – with tons of tenderness."

JOE MONKMAN, Personal Development Trainer

"*The Destiny Roadmap* provides seekers of liberation from fear a pathway to peace. Kelli Reese skillfully invites the reader to navigate The Void and traverse their inner landscape to mind the mind and embrace their pure potentiality. In the wise words of Joseph Campbell, follow your bliss and allow the wisdom distilled from Kelli's journey to become a touchstone for your own path of self transformation. With practical steps and real time examples of her client's stories, you will feel empowered to change your life with ease and grace!"

PEGGY FARMER, PHD,
Author of *Exploratory Surgery of the Soul: A Journey to Self Mastery*

"Must-read for all who experience fear and want an actionable solution that will free them from it. Kelli's acronym for fear is brilliant and unforgettable. She shares her personal story of applying it and experiencing her own transformational shift to move beyond fear and now shares her process with you so you can, too."

MARSHA-KAY FARIAS,
International Bestselling Author of *Everyday Medium*

THE DESTINY ROADMAP

*The Little Guidebook to Face
Your Fears, Embrace Change,
and Follow Your Heart*

KELLI REESE

NEW YORK

LONDON • NASHVILLE • MELBOURNE • VANCOUVER

THE DESTINY ROADMAP

Published in New York, New York, by Morgan James Publishing in partnership with Difference Press.
www.MorganJamesPublishing.com

The Morgan James Speakers Group can bring authors to your live event. For more information or to book an event visit The Morgan James Speakers Group at www.TheMorganJamesSpeakersGroup.com.

ISBN 978-1-68350-729-1 paperback
ISBN 978-1-68350-730-7 eBook
Library of Congress Control Number: 2017912926

Interior Design by:
Megan Whitney
Creative Ninja Designs
megan@creativeninjadesigns.com

In an effort to support local communities, raise awareness and funds, Morgan James Publishing donates a percentage of all book sales for the life of each book to Habitat for Humanity Peninsula and Greater Williamsburg.

Get involved today! Visit
www.MorganJamesBuilds.com

For anyone who has ever considered walking away
and stared across the dark abyss,
wondering what, if anything, is on the other side.

CONTENTS

INTRODUCTION

"Here is a test to see if your mission on earth
is finished: if you're alive, it isn't."

RICHARD BACH, *Illusions*

There's a place we can find ourselves in life where one door closes and another has yet to open. I call this place The Void. It's an unfamiliar place, since we're not accustomed to being there often. It can feel overwhelming, vast, and uncomfortable, especially when the door shut on something that used to have meaning, like a job or a relationship.

We come into The Void with a mixed bag of emotions, feeling like we're on unsteady ground. It's like trying to stand on a life raft with a tiny hole in it. The raft is our only security, and it's slowly deflating. We don't want to fall in, but little by little, our support system is dissolving. Water slowly ripples onto our lifeline; looking down we feel helpless as the water pools around our ankles, and the raft melts away and crumples. We have no idea what to do. We're terrified; it feels like the end to everything we've known. *This is not how it's supposed to be; I didn't sign on for this; I better figure out what the hell I'm doing.*

All this happens when we walk through the door into The Void. We don't even know where we are, but we have the impression that it's not right and that we need to get moving immediately, or we're in deep trouble. We're scared, and we don't know where to turn, so we instinctively head toward what's familiar – typically, what's behind us in the rearview mirror.

We can be in The Void for months, even years, and not realize it's a hollow abyss. We can be stuck in the place of "should I stay or should I go," working diligently on our pros and cons, weighing the gravity of what a decision either way, means. We attempt to forecast the outcome like a business deal, so we land gently, but it feels like we're trying to jump out of an airplane without a parachute. Even though we have no clue what to do or where we want to be, we've been mentally working hard to leave a situation we find hard to unravel: a situation that's sucking the light out of our eyes.

We're unaware of this at first. The fear of walking away has us in a fog. We can't get clarity on a path forward, so we stay where we are. Here's the thing to understand: when we're in that painful place of indecision and we anchor ourselves to a life that no longer fits, we're already in The Void.

When we want to let go and do something that feels more aligned with our heart and soul, something less stressful or draining, we're already in The Void. When our soul is screaming at us to get moving already, but we're stalling because we're paralyzed with doubt, we're already in The Void.

Intelligent and often outwardly successful women end up in The Void. In fact, we all identify with the idea that, when looking back on the experience that brought us there, we instinctively felt something grabbing for our attention, almost like we were being pulled to walk away from where we were, no matter how successful, smart, or outwardly "right" that place appeared to be. Many times we pushed away that magnetic feeling that we were meant to be doing something different somewhere else, because we were afraid to walk away from the known into the unknown, no matter how much pain we were in.

At some point, it becomes too much to bear, and there's no other option but to move on. Even though we're apprehensive, we realize we must take action in spite of the doubt. At first, we can feel an incredible sense of freedom when we make the decision to walk further into The Void and close the door behind us. There's a release, because we finally made a decision. We left behind something that was feeling like it had overstayed its welcome.

When we make a choice to remove ourselves from the pain of where we were in exchange for the unchartered Void, we take the first amazing step toward living a better life. It takes courage to face our fear and walk away when we're scared. Never underestimate the power behind that first step.

When the elation wanes and the reality of where we are sets in, the journey through The Void can take us on an emotional rollercoaster ride. Fear slides into the driver's seat and rams us into seemingly unavoidable road blocks.

What is it with fear anyway? How often have we let fear decide where we're going, how we're living, or when we're going to allow our voice to actually *have* a voice? We let fear drop in, and it feels as real as burning ourselves on a hot stove: shocking, with a lasting sear. That's when we feel the emotional fall into a butt-trembling mind freeze. It's all-consuming, and our first instinct is to run like hell, thinking if we remove ourselves from the circumstances and find a safe place to hide we'll be ok: the anxiety will subside. But The Void is all around us. It's where we are, and there is no escaping its immense vacuum. It requires us to make decisions and take action in order to find the door out. We can't hide in The Void if we want to move forward into a new chapter without dragging the old life and the previous person we were with us. We need to wipe the slate, even though we're fearful.

Fear is the killer of dreams. Fear is the murderer of lightness. Fear is the destroyer of wishes and hopes. In reality, fear stops us in our tracks precisely because it doesn't want us to make deadly mistakes. It's just looking out for us, only it rises up when we often need it to chill in the background and make a move only when we're really in danger. Fear and insecurity can silently rule our lives even when it seems, on the outside, like we've got it all under control. The idea of control is an illusion; when we insist on control, that's when fear has its strongest hold on us. We hold on so tightly that we fear losing influence in our lives, and in that space, fear is controlling our lives at every turn.

Once we've surrendered to The Void, we realize we can't go back, but many of us keep looking in the rearview mirror anyway, because it's painfully secure. For others of us, what was isn't there anymore as an option, so we knuckle down and push forward, gripped with uncertainty. But first we have to make the arduous decision to let go.

What if letting go was actually the hardest part of the entire process? What if wrestling with confusion and trying to make the right decision could be the most painful experience we have in The Void? What if the unknown wasn't a vast scary nothingness to fear?

Would it make it easier to walk away?

I want to show you that it's possible to embrace the fear and walk out of The Void with clarity, peace, and excitement about where we're headed. That it's possible to create a roadmap that leads us directly to our soul's destiny. That we can have a deeper understanding about where we've been and what we're doing here.

This book is about what we can do, once we let go, to make our way through The Void into the next phase of a life of our own making, a life based on our passions and our soul's gifts. It's not always easy, but it's possible to discover how to be completely in love with our life when we take advantage of our time in The Void and the gift it offers. We can embrace the unknown with open arms and a smile, because we're on a path creating a roadmap to a life that's in alignment with our deepest desires, our soul's calling.

We might only recognize this calling as a whisper at first, but the faint call turns into a grueling yell once we've ignored it for longer than is healthy. Typically it's an unforgettable feeling that's grabbing for our attention, calling us to be somewhere other than where we are. This is the Soul Calling, and when we finally decide to answer the call, it becomes a pull we can embrace and connect to clearly and easily. As we make our way toward our truest self and our dreams, we become stronger and more grounded. We're in a place of creating a life we're excited to wake up to every morning: a life of our wildest dreams.

Even though the calling is soft at first, the soul's whisper can become as clear and familiar as our best friend's reassuring voice on the other end of the phone after a long day. It can become the trusted consultant we look to without a second thought. It can become our partner and decision-maker, the co-creator of our Destiny Roadmap.

The Void can be our moment to pause, release, and recalibrate, so when we open the door on the other side, we step into the incredible place we've imagined, explored, and birthed. If we do the work required, it's possible to embrace The Void with confidence, courage, and a light heart. It's possible to face and confront the fears that are ultimately standing in the way of where we're meant to be, our destiny.

Chapter 1
THIS IS NOT MY BEAUTIFUL LIFE

Athena thought she was really good at working with people, but then her professional relationships kept falling apart. She thought, *maybe I'm not as good as I think I am.* She questioned herself constantly, never really considering it might be where she was, not who she was.

Tina had a gnawing feeling of internal discomfort that became omnipresent. Frequent disagreements with her partner became increasingly difficult, emotionally. *I felt the pain and anxiety deep in my heart. Often I felt so sad and out of place in my own home, despite being surrounded by all I'd known for years.*

Brandi felt some things were improving in her job, but they didn't outweigh what wasn't. She encountered negativity on a daily basis, and it weighed heavily on her heart. *I believed I could make everything better, that I could make people happy. I worked in an extremely tough environment where the dissenting culture was anti-management.* She had good intentions and wanted the best for everyone. She believed with enough accountability, improvements, and the right people in place, her workplace could become a happy place. But for her, it didn't, and she brought the stress home every day. It impacted every relationship she had, but it still took a long time before she made the decision to walk away.

Does this sound familiar?

Are you experiencing what it's like to feel anchored somewhere that no longer makes you happy and fulfilled?

I too know what it's like to live in a place that no longer speaks to your soul. You look around and feel like everyone else has it all figured out, and what's swirling around in your head vacillates between *it's not that bad* and *what the hell am I doing?* To add to the stress, there's this nagging feeling that you're being pushed in a completely different direction without a roadmap or GPS. You're resistant, and the fear is paralyzing.

From the outside looking in, your life seems pretty good, yet you feel that unavoidable draw, that distant voice, saying, *there's more to it than just this.* You feel unfulfilled, and it's hard to enjoy what you have. You want to make changes, but you don't know how or where to start.

You truly believe if you could just stop worrying so much, you might be able to think more clearly and find some direction. You feel stuck and uninspired. If you had to pinpoint anything, you're pretty sure fear is holding you back and preventing you from making any changes at all; you recognize it because you've felt its presence in your life all too often. You continually push it away in favor of staying where you are, even though that place is acutely and increasingly uncomfortable.

You're scared you've made the wrong decisions in life, and it's too late to do something about it. This can be a laundry list of anything: I shouldn't have chosen the men I did. I should have walked away from this job by now. I had different plans for myself. I should have left this relationship, city, stress, years ago. Underlying all of it is the bigger question, *why am I staying somewhere so painful?*

You frequently look at other people and admire their _____ (insert your word here: peace, happiness, relationship, contentment, smile, laughter), whatever you feel is missing in your life. You wish desperately that someone would just tell you how to get *it*, because where you are is excruciatingly heavy, and you miss lightness, spirit, and laughter. It feels like you have decisions to make, but you're completely mystified about what to do, so you continue to stick it out because, when you look over the horizon of perceived opportunities, nothing speaks to your heart. When you peek out from behind your safety net, the scene is terrifying.

There's a constant chatter in your mind telling you conflicting messages about why it's fine to stick around, why it's best not to make any changes right now. But the pain, *that pain*, is palpable. It lives on the edge of your emotions. It tugs at your heart, and it factors into everything you do. Even though you convince yourself otherwise, there's something inside you pulsing and wanting: a deep desire to find out what's calling you and an even deeper desire to extract yourself from your own denial.

And can we just talk about your heart for a minute? I know it's the biggest weight you're pulling around. When you have the courage to connect to it, your heart feels unsupported, untrusting, and shut down – bottom line, it feels like a 100-pound weight is dangling from it by a meat hook. If it could fall from where it is, it would definitely fall into the pit in your stomach to join up with that gaping hole that wants to be filled with something you can't explain. You absolutely *know* that hole isn't looking for your heart on a meat hook, but other than that, you're at a loss.

How did you get here? It seemed like everything was on track. For a number of years you were excited about your life – at times, even passionate. You woke up feeling happy, as if you were on the right path at the right time with the right people, doing the right thing. You're wondering where it all went and how you ended up feeling so disconnected from your joy. The more you try to make it all fit, the more painful it becomes. It's like squeezing into a pair of jeans two sizes too small. You can still get in them, but once you're in, you can't move comfortably and some areas are spilling out all over, and that's embarrassing. So you try to gather that stuff up and shove it back in, or worse, mask it so no one else can see it – *out of sight, out of mind*. Only, it's not out of your mind. You feel it oozing out, and you hope no one notices. You hope you're hiding it all so well that no one asks how they can help you, because you don't even know where to start.

For a while you've been successful at making it all ok, mostly for everyone else. You've made the world around them fit the world around you so you don't upset the balance. No one really knows where you are, you've become accustomed to deep breaths and looking up to stop the tears from falling. The darn tears are the tipping point. They reside at the back of your throat, and once they get rolling, you need to duck out to get things back in order. You can't quite figure out the trigger, but you know it has something to do with feeling like you're in exactly the wrong place and the longer you stay there, the more you feel yourself shutting down.

Most importantly, you instinctively feel like a door has already closed on where you are. You've felt like this for longer than you care to admit, but your heart and head are not aligned with walking away. It's painful and the emotions are raw. When you think about making a move, you feel trapped by the circumstances you're in and the reality of what it would mean to make a change, especially right now. The timing just isn't right, so you try to lose some weight so the jeans fit better, so you're comfortable in your life, because you can come up with a hundred reasons why it's not as bad as it seems, why the misery of your present is better than the fear of an unplanned future.

You're smart, you've accomplished quite a bit in your life, but your friends and family regularly check in, because they've noticed a shift. You're not as upbeat as you were, you're tired all the time. You do a stellar job of redirecting and making sure your feelings aren't the topic of conversation, because you're not accustomed to breaking down outside the quiet warmth of your vehicle or behind the closed door of your bedroom. You don't want to reveal more about what you're truly feeling, because if you start talking about how horrified you are, how it feels like your soul is slowly dying, and how if you had the choice to walk away from your life and it wouldn't disrupt anyone too much, then you might just take the next train out ... except you're scared, because you don't know where the train is headed.

When you look within, your biggest challenge is overcoming the recurring feeling that you're not connected to anything worthwhile. The fear that comes up when you admit that to yourself, is unmistakable. Fear is holding you back in so many ways, it creates a crippling stagnation that arises at incredibly inappropriate times. It has you feeling wedged in a corner. You want to come out fighting, but it wins more often that you'd like.

Your fear isn't always in the forefront, but it's not a good fear either, like the one that comes when you're going to jump out of an airplane – not that you've done that. Although, you can imagine *that* fear comes with some excitement, because you've decided to do something scary, and *that* fear, you figure, is thrilling and probably welcome. Your fear is much less glamorous. Your fear manifests as concern, worry, distress, aversion, anxiety – it's break-out-in-sweat fear. You feel it when you think about taking those jeans off and finding some that fit more comfortably, but you detest trying on jeans, because you have to go through 30 pair to find one that fits. It's too exhausting, and you're required to spend way too much time looking at yourself in a mirror.

At some point you catch yourself with an uncontrollable desire to lash out at co-workers, friends, or family because everything they do drives. you. crazy. You don't recognize the angry person hiding inside you. The deep breath strategy no longer helps you find patience, which is troubling. You hate yourself for getting mad in the first place, because you're a genuinely caring person.

I understand.

This place is agonizing, it's absolutely one of the most painful places to be. Your soul is screaming, *just get out already,* and the noise is deafening. You feel trapped in indecision even though you've had continual, nagging thoughts that you're not where you're meant to be. The pain of staying where you are seems better than regretting the decision to walk away, but there's an explanation for the anguish. The reason it's so painful is that you haven't consciously made the decision to move forward and recognize that the door has already closed on a life that no longer fits.

Here's the thing, *the decision has already been made.* I promise you, it's true. Deep within your heart and soul, you've decided. Theoretically, you're already in The Void, You just haven't realized it yet. That's why you're in so much pain. The good news is, the story you've created, about what will happen to you when you make a decision to walk away from the very thing that is crushing your soul, is way bigger than what it's actually like. I assure you, the reality of it isn't as bad as your fear wants you to believe. The divide between where you are and where you're meant to be, is not as wide as your mind tells you it is.

You're imagining it will feel like you've been forced on a stage naked with blinding spotlights, and you don't have a script. You can feel everyone staring at you, waiting for you. That fear of feeling so vulnerable without any support or guidance is what keeps you from walking away. That fear of the unknown is what keeps you from finally making the decision. Bottom line, you were right: fear *is* holding you back and preventing you from making any decisions at all. But it's ok. That's why you're here reading this book. That's what I want to help you understand, that it's ok to make a move and walk away into the unknown, even though you're terrified. That you don't have to stay where it no longer clicks.

Here's a question to consider. If you don't walk away, and then you find yourself right here five years from now, *how will you feel?* If you start reading this book again and realize you're in exactly the same place, but the pain is more extreme and everything is magnified x100, *what will that feel like?* What will you have told yourself over those years about what you're capable of? How much pain will you have stuffed away into those jeans?

If you decide to stay here in the suffering, what are you telling yourself about having a deep longing for something more? What are you saying about that desire to feel connected to something? What message are you sending to the fear inside? You're saying it wins. And honestly, that's exactly what it wants. Your fear is fighting for you to stay safe and comfortable. It doesn't want you to let go and figure out where you're meant to be. When we take scary but positive steps toward the unknown, fear decides to roll up its sleeves and get serious. It says, *what were you thinking? You made a decision without a plan,* and with that, *we* start to second guess ourselves, because we believe we don't know where we're headed.

Here's a trick: think about walking away. Now check in. You can probably feel some fear, but doesn't that fear feel different, like the fear you imagined a newbie skydiver feels when they were getting ready to jump out of the plane? Sure, there's some of the familiar fear you know so well, but it's mixed with excitement, isn't it? I know, it can still be paralyzing, because we like to know the plan, and we like to feel in control. But mixed in is anticipation, because you're finally considering what it means to unshackle yourself, even though the path is unknown.

When you officially decide to walk away into The Void and close the door behind you, fear will have a heyday, because it thinks you don't have a plan. But you will have a plan. You will put fear on notice, and this book will show you how.

What if you could let go and gain all the direction you desire? What if it's possible to make your way through The Void with confidence? What if you could make choices you don't question? What if you could find what's been calling you all this time, that pull you've felt toward something more, something unidentifiable?

I can't promise the fear and uncomfortable emotions we experience in The Void will completely go away when you let go and move forward.

In fact I can pretty much say they won't. What I can promise is that it's more than possible to embrace your fears instead of hiding from them, and you can learn to make courageous choices based in fulfillment rather than fear. You can learn to create an incredible life out of a dark place. There's an incredible payoff for trusting in what you can't yet see in The Void.

It's possible to feel excited to get up each day, because you have clarity about where you're headed. It's possible to feel positive and confident in your choices, knowing you're on the right path. You're calmer, because you're receiving validation for your dreams, and you're seeing glimpses of what it can be like on the other side of The Void. You begin to understand what it means to see your path ahead and have no question about where you're going and why. It's possible to have a roadmap to show you the way. A roadmap that aligns with your soul. This is your Destiny Roadmap.

It's painful now, because you haven't let go completely and walked into the unknown. It's possible to make the choice to embrace it all, fear included, and savor the time you spend in The Void, co-creating a life you love with your soul and the Universe.

This book will show you how.

Chapter 2
IT'S JUST ANOTHER GROWTH OPPORTUNITY

T hat's me on a life-changing trip to Tulum in February, 2016; I'm on top of the tallest pyramid at Coba, an archaeological site in the Yucatán Peninsula. The Nohuch Mul (which means "large mound" in the Mayan language) pyramid is more  than 130 feet in height, roughly equivalent to a 14-story building (accounting for the fact that the 13th floor is typically omitted).

I'm not one to go scaling the outside of a multi-story building; frankly, heights toss my insides around.

At the bottom, looking up, I wracked my neck trying to see the top. I ignored the fact that the people up there looked like tiny ants atop an ant hill. My mind was full of every single reason why I shouldn't climb the pyramid. *You're afraid of heights.* Yes, I am. *Your husband is back in California; what if something bad happens?* Anything is possible, I peeped. *If you go up there, you have to come down.* Ugh! The dread in that thought was substantial, as I recalled memories where fear took me over at much lower heights.

Once my husband Joe and I were driving up 13,000-foot peaks in Silverton, CO. As we inched our way up, the road got steeper and narrower. Then the car stalled, and we started sliding backwards toward the bottom. Instinctively, I shoved my foot into the brake so hard I thought it might go through the floor, but we continued the descent, trying to avoid the huge drop-off on the left. I panicked. My body was flooded with terror as tears filled my eyes, making it difficult to see. I was not the picture of grace under pressure, but I was in the driver's seat, and I had to get my act together, get the car in gear, and start moving forward on a steep mountain. *I can't do it!* I shouted through my tears. Joe was calm and collected, as usual. He said, in a matter of fact manner, *Calm down, yes, you can. It's ok.* I think I even heard him give a slight chuckle. I wanted to punch him for not understanding the deadly situation we were in, for seeming unfazed by the fact that we were sliding backwards down a narrow dirt road at 13,000 feet, and the driver was in a tizzy. When we finally slid to a stop, I took stock of where we were, gazing up the steep road from where we came. I knew we had to move, so I took a deep breath and put all my focus on the next right step. I powered through my fear, even though my legs were shaking, and my head was a blur. It was an incredible lesson in pushing through, in spite of the fear.

I haven't always been afraid of heights. It's something I picked up along the way. It's a story I told myself to give me an excuse for why I couldn't do something. Usually, Joe was with me, and I'd have his calm voice to lean on, but he wasn't with me at the bottom of the towering pyramid. *What if I panic in the middle of going up and freeze? What if I find the courage to get up there, freak out, and can't make it back down?* I was deep in the throes of self-doubt, and the only thing to hold onto besides breakfast in my stomach was a thick rope laying on the steps someone put there for security. It could've broken any time. My mind has always had an incredible knack for thinking of the worst that could happen in any moment. It never failed. Even when things were going well.

A Mayan guide I chatted with earlier interrupted my thoughts, he must have seen the look on my face. *You going to climb the big pyramid?* The accent blanketed his English perfectly. His voice was comforting. Out of my mouth came, *Oh, yes! I'm doing it all!* What? *Who the hell was that?* It was a voice I hadn't heard for a long time. An unhesitating voice. It knew I had to climb the pyramid, no matter how scared I was. I'd always had an internal coach who was on my side, but I hadn't allowed her to chime in much over the last few years, so when she found her way out, I was surprised.

I looked back at the towering pyramid and noticed my traveling companions already at the top, sitting on the edge enjoying the view and obviously unafraid of heights. I was feeling the familiar sickness in my stomach just seeing them when my inner coach piped up: *If you make it up there, at least you'll have support; that's something.* So I started to ask myself a few questions as I stood at the bottom like a little girl looking up at her father and waiting for him to tell her it's all going to be ok. *Did you not come all this way to find yourself again?* Yes, I absolutely did. Check that box in favor of the climb. *You can see other people navigating it and not perishing, right?* Yes, another checked box. The most important question: *How will you feel if you walk away, and you don't do this?* That one hit deep in my soul. I had asked the right question at the right time that nudged me across the dividing line between *hell no* and *what have I got to lose*. This was an important lesson that would serve me well as I made my way through The Void.

Only look at what's in front of you; don't worry about coming back down; take it one step at a time. And most of all smile. What? *Smile*, the voice inside me said, *because honey, you're doing it.*

I knew this was a turning point in my life; it was something I had to seize. I understood the importance of the trip to Tulum without my husband. I comprehended the significance of the experience and what it would mean if I could push through my crippling fear and do this thing. And with an internal *holy crap*, I walked up to the bottom step, took a deep breath, put a smile on my face, and started to climb on all fours, making my way toward the top with focused determination.

Halfway up, I managed to strike up a conversation with two women coming down on their butts. *Is it worth it?* I reluctantly asked, looking for moral support. *Meh*, said the first lady, but before that thought landed anywhere in my world, the other lady yelled with enthusiasm, *Oh, yes! Even if you have to come down on your butt.* I blurted out, *But I'm afraid of heights! So am I*, she said emphatically. *OK, thank you!* I yelled as I smiled wider and pushed forward. We can often get a little gift of encouragement when we're smack dab in our own noise, swirling in fear. We just need to be open to asking for it and receiving it in unlikely places. Her words gave me the courage I needed to forge ahead, and I never looked back.

Making it to the top of that pyramid was a defining moment in my search and subsequent mission to reclaim myself, the *me* I had lost in the previous few years. The one who became smaller in the experience that brought me into The Void. I knew climbing that pyramid was an important piece of the puzzle. I didn't know what was on top, but I was certain I had to push through the fear and intimidation and dig deep to get my butt up there.

Even though I was rewarded with a breathtaking view and the most incredible sense of accomplishment, I know now the journey itself was equally as important as standing on top. I couldn't believe I did it. I conquered the fear. I immediately called my friend and mentor, Peggy. She's the one who told me if I was going to Tulum, I had to make it to Coba. She had never steered me wrong in the 15 years I've known her loving support and friendship. I shared my excitement with her about Coba, the pyramid, and especially my heart! I knew she would get it, because she's all about the heart.

When I arrived on top, I felt my heart expand. Through embracing my fear and climbing the pyramid, my heart blew open. It was so unexpected. I had no idea I would connect so deeply to my spirit and love on top of a pyramid in the Yucatan, but this is how it happens when we decide we're sick and tired of letting fear stop us from living an amazing life and holding us back from who we're meant to be. This is where I received the first glimpse of the Destiny Roadmap. This is where I discovered how important it is to embrace our lives in spite of debilitating fears.

Two months before that decisive moment at the bottom of the pyramid in Coba, I'd walked away from a six-figure job without a concrete plan for what to do next. At the time, I was heavy-hearted, exhausted, and generally not myself. What I knew was the job was feeling more like a battle every day. I was waking up, dreading the thought of facing the militia. The positive parts, the parts I *loved* about the job, were no longer outweighing the negative parts. The role no longer completely aligned with my soul, and it was devastating to admit, because there were so many good parts that did. *How could I walk away?*

It was hard to come to the inevitable conclusion that it was time to break free. I had spent 20 years working my way along a path in the natural foods industry, first as an entrepreneur and then in the world of grocery. I loved everything about it. I worked my way up in natural foods markets, culminating with the last few years spent as the GM of a $34-million organization. I followed my path to a job where I thought I could settle in and make a comfortable living. Even though it was stressful, the work was gratifying, because I felt like I was making a difference. Until it all came crashing down.

For a long time, I didn't want to admit something was off, but I was working with a leadership coach because I wanted to be sure I had tried everything to make my round peg fit in the square hole of that job. During that time, I focused on the work of the position and the work of myself, and I took it all in. The day finally came when I had to answer the question my coach proposed months earlier: *What if this is happening for you and not to you?* I knew she was right. It's a question I had already considered deep inside my heart. I felt like I wasn't where I was meant to be any longer. I felt a deeper calling, but I pushed it aside, over and over again, because so much of the job felt right and because so many people were relying on me to come through. It was hard to let go, but instinctively, I knew it was all unfolding in a piercing and anguished way so there would be no mistaking the outcome I was being reluctantly pushed toward.

It wasn't the first time I'd received confirmation that I wasn't where I was meant to be. This has happened a number of times over the years, and I usually answered the call with clarity and vigor. But something had changed. I was different in that job. I seemed to have lost my confidence, my joy, and, worst of all, my spirit.

When I finally admitted to myself what was truly happening, the bottom dropped out quickly. In short, I was pushed into The Void, because I had no choice but to walk away.

To this day, people are still confused about why I left, because I chose to keep it within a small core group of those involved or who needed to know. I didn't answer the many inquiries from the local paper about what happened, because I'd learned over the years that it wasn't easy for me to express what was truly going on in a quoted blurb in the paper. I came to understand that no matter what I said, it wouldn't change anything. But truthfully, most people couldn't care less about what was happening at the organization where *I* was concerned. When the announcement came out in the paper that I had resigned, I said to myself, *Must be a slow news day.* It was the first step in releasing myself from the experience. Sure, there were negative comments on the story, but it didn't matter what anyone thought they knew about what happened. My decision was my own, and I didn't need anyone to validate it for me. It was the first time in three years that a spark of my spirit returned.

Later every decision I had made prior to walking away haunted me and held me hostage in a way I never expected, but I figured out that there was an important message for me as I journeyed through The Void. That is what this book is about, and that is why I'm telling you my story. I know you can relate, and I hope it will help you decide that it's important to answer the call even though you might be scared and that you don't have to wait another minute to decide. I figured out how to embrace this unknown place I call The Void and make it work for me rather than the other way around, and I want to show you how to do that too.

When it all came crashing down, I had three large fibroid tumors growing inside my uterus and chronic pain in my coccyx. I wasn't sleeping through the night since I was usually lost in a cycle of cogitating and worrying. In those dark moments before the world around me awoke, my mind would take over with cryptic scenes and self-judgment. Everything was out of my control, and I was beating myself up for being so shortsighted. Worrying incessantly can be one of the most challenging things we encounter in The Void; we're going to talk about this in Chapter 10 – Mind the Mind. I've got you covered.

This wasn't my first trip through The Void. I've been there a number of times before. Each time with varying degrees of pain and triumph. All equally glorious, messy, and humbling.

When I was 26, I went through a period of intense transformation, like an Extreme Makeover Home Edition on steroids, only this was for my insides. I walked away from a job I despised, my mom died from cancer at 63, and I got sober. Not necessarily in that order, but all equally life-altering. During that time, I experienced the deepest, darkest longing for something I never really understood or knew. I learned how to laugh through excruciating pain and how to show up when I didn't want to. I learned the meaning of *the only way around it is through it,* and I let go through an overwhelming process of grieving while strengthening my connection to spirit and in turn, myself. I found that connection in the most unlikely place for me – in the rooms of Alcoholics Anonymous (AA).

I'd always been a big partier in my teens, and that carried over into my 20s while living in New York City. In 1995, I was invited to hear a friend speak at an AA meeting. While there, I heard someone else talking about their drinking, and it sounded eerily familiar. While looking around the room to avoid eye contact, I noticed The 12 Steps on a huge poster. The third step stood out to me: *Made a decision to turn our will and our lives over to the care of God, <u>as we understood Him.</u>* The word God in the third step stood out; it reverberated through my body. Why *God* resonated with me at that moment was puzzling. I wasn't raised religiously; I really was the most unlikely person to embrace God. I remember thinking, *I'm missing God in my life? God is going to fill the cavernous hole in the pit of my stomach?* That seemed way too simple and extremely cheesy. But on that day, in that meeting, listening to that speaker talk about her life with drugs and alcohol, I started to believe that maybe she was onto something; maybe all the people in that meeting were onto something. For some reason everything seemed to make sense, and the other people in the room appeared to be happy: something I was not. I was miserable, and I wanted what those AA people had: authenticity and comfort in their own skin. If AA gave them that, I was in, because what I'd been doing clearly wasn't working.

I'd been asking seemingly unanswerable questions for years. *What is wrong with me? What am I doing here? Why do I feel so empty?* In that moment, in that room, it occurred to me that I had finally received the direction I needed to figure out the answers. I didn't question the *how*, I just decided to embrace the *what:* AA. It would be a lesson that would serve me well for years to come, and we'll discuss its importance in The Void in Chapter 3 – *Direct Your Drive.*

I threw myself into AA, feeling like I was finally headed in the right direction. I wasn't sure if I was an alcoholic, really, but for the first time I truly felt a part of something: that I belonged somewhere. Then it all got overwhelmingly real. When I had 60 days in the program, my mom died, and my world crumbled around me like a building being intentionally demolished. I thought I was low before I walked into AA, but the weight of the grief taught me otherwise, and yet, I took on more.

I don't know if it was my mom's death or the fact that I was coming out of a long haze into sobriety, but at that same time, I walked away from a job I despised on Wall Street. Each day the elevator doors would open to the lobby of the investment firm where I worked, and I'd want to throw up. It had been clear I should leave for a long time, but the money was so good that I ignored the blatant sexual harassment, sexism, and verbal abuse I witnessed or experienced regularly. Leaving that job was my first taste of liberation. It was another instance where I instinctively made a choice I knew to be right, even though I had no idea how it would work out. I just knew I couldn't do it anymore. It was my first journey into The Void: plain and simple and scary as hell.

Once I quit the job, I put the focus on myself and on staying sober through the sorrow and heartbreak of losing my mom. I'd raise my hand in meetings and let people know what I was going through. Some days, people would offer support. And other days, they wouldn't. Those *wouldn't* days, I'd feel like an open wound, exposed and weak, thinking everyone was judging me. Of course, they weren't, but my mind sent me into deep darkness. Learning to tame that critic was another tool I called upon in my quest to make my way through The Void. It's an important part of the steps that we're going to look at more closely as we move forward.

Looking back, I can see that I was willing to do the work in AA because I was in so much pain. It was an agonizing yet reflective time for me. Oftentimes I felt desperate and panic-stricken. I'd talk myself through it or call my sponsor and ask for help. I hated asking for help. It made me feel vulnerable and weak, but I did it anyway.

If you spend enough time at AA meetings, eventually you come across someone whose story makes yours look like a cake walk. This happened for me around the six-month mark when my dear friend

Karen and I were inspired to go to a different meeting. We were both newly sober and feeling equally pathetic, so we decided to switch it up. The speaker was a man with a soft, angelic voice. He was inspiring, hopeful, and heartbreaking. He was dying of AIDS. This was in the mid-90s just before the cocktail, when people were still seeing AIDS as a death sentence.

I was mesmerized as I listened to his story with tears running down my cheeks. His words rode on an arrow across the packed room, straight into my being. I hung on every syllable. I wanted to wrap myself up in the comfort of his understanding. I wanted to have the courage to see beauty even though I was scared. I wanted to find gratitude in my own darkness, just like him. At the end of the meeting, we went up to thank him like groupies at a concert. He was generous with his energy; he seemed to care about the six-month's sober groupies in front of him more than the fact that he had just changed our lives with his story, with his words. If someone dying could be so positive and offer so much hope, then what was I doing feeling pity for myself and my situation? It was in that moment that I pivoted. I began living in tune with where my life was going; working to control it all less and *Let Go and Let God*, a well-known AA slogan. It's when I decided to show up differently. My pain didn't disappear by any means, but I embraced it and channeled it into my growth.

My library of books on spirituality grew exponentially. I devoured title after title that spoke to me. I spent hours in the Midtown Barnes and Noble with Karen, sitting on the floor in the spirituality section flipping pages, receiving the messages we felt were meant expressly for us. We were kids in a candy store. It was more of a re-awakening, as I was unlocking everything I already knew, and the authors of the books I picked up knew it too. I was connecting to my truth; with my heart. That is the foundation of this book, and that is how it's possible to find the way out of The Void. I'll show you it's ok to trust in the process of the steps and our connection to the Universe.

I have a vivid memory of a perfectly warm New York City day, walking down the street with friends on the Upper West Side. In a brief moment, everything around me came together as one. It was a feeling that enveloped all my senses. I felt that I was a whole part of the beingness of that moment. I was completely one with everything, which sounds New Age-y, but it's true. Through working on myself and being of service to others, I was finding my way out, I was finding brief flashes of unbelievable peace. This was my official spiritual awakening. With friends, I began attending parties that centered around meditation, spiritual talks, past-life regression, and enlightenment. Growing up, I had experiences with the metaphysical realm, but I had no one in my life who showed me the way, so it wasn't nurtured, and it came and went. The alcohol and drugs worked to muddle my spiritual path, but AA brought me back to it... and then beyond it.

Three years after I walked into the bubble of AA, I walked back out into the world. I came to the realization that I wasn't an alcoholic. It was clear to me that I'd been led to AA to realize my connection to spirit, to survive my mother's death with unending support, and to get honest and find forgiveness for myself. Those three years transformed my life, and leaving the security of the program and my friends was crushing and frightening. I knew if I stayed I would always rely on the safety and comfort of where I was. When I added in the fact that I knew I didn't have an addiction to alcohol, I decided to walk away, into the unknown. I chose The Void again.

Even though I was a more grounded and connected human on the planet, everything was not rainbows and unicorns. In between moments of clarity, it was awkward, complex, and complicated. I fell down a lot. I gained an advanced degree in pep talks, determination, and first aid for my soul. I had to answer for every choice I made, and I grappled with the consequences. I also voluntarily chose The Void a number of additional times, but each with less pain involved on the front end. Every decision I made, I learned to make with more and more confidence. The constant? I was dedicated to learning and my spiritual growth, period!

I didn't do it fearlessly. In fact there were times I clung so deeply to the illusion of control I thought I might spontaneously combust. There were times I beat myself up so hard for every little thing I did that I thought the bruises must be visible. And yet I kept going. I asked questions and I remained steadfast to the unending search for a way to peace. I wanted to find my way back to that brief moment in time where I captured the being-ness on the street in NYC. I had this idea that if I could retain that experience for longer than a bleep in time, I would be set free.

So I spent the next 20 years on a path of self-discovery. I explored everything from energy work to yoga. I left NYC to move to North Carolina. I sold cookware on the road at home and garden shows; I was engulfed in a turbulent relationship. I got to know my inner child, and she was pissed. I studied for a year with a Lakota Shaman. I worked with a life coach and I spent time in my garden. I was regularly paralyzed by fear and answered back over and over again, gaining more strength each time.

Eventually, I explored the fine art of showing up for a healthy relationship when I met my husband in North Carolina. We followed my career path through three different states. With each move, I gained more understanding of following where led, listening to guidance, and creating a life that aligned with my soul. I began to see my experiences, including the hard times, as *just another growth opportunity*. All these experiences helped me create The Destiny Roadmap Framework; unbeknownst to me, it was the first puzzle piece of co-creating my own way out of The Void.

When it was time for me to walk away from the natural foods job that was crushing my spirit, the one that had been supporting the life we'd become accustomed to, my husband Joe was the first in line to say, *It will be ok.* He always says, *It's just money; we'll make more.* In his most supportive way, he gave me the freedom and space to go on the trip to Tulum to find myself again and return home to spend a year in The Void differently than I'd ever done before. At that time, I had no idea that my trip to Tulum would provide so many answers to questions I was struggling with. I didn't know it would be the trip of a lifetime.

I never doubted the gift of The Void, but I didn't realize I was being called to do something more than what I'd been doing and reach more people than I was exposed to in my job. To become who I was supposed to be next and not buy into the fear unconditionally. To take advantage of the time and forge a new path. My trip to Tulum was the starting point.

The journey has been about re-discovery, trust, and letting go. I'd never spent time reviewing some of the tools and lessons I'd learned over the years, so I became reflective and created a path for myself to follow. When I got back from Tulum, I set some intentions and I made commitments, just like we're going to do in Chapter 3 – *Direct Your Drive.* I followed the stepping stones to a new life and into a new me. I was so successful with the 12-step program more than 20 years ago, I knew having steps in place to guide me would be the secret sauce to my success.

There were challenges, of course. There always are. So I created tools for those too. It all came together in the most magical way, and because I was outlining a course of action to follow, I felt more confident in the process.

I'd been helping people follow their hearts for years through friendships, client relationships, or work with employees. Once I figured out how to do it all differently in The Void, it seemed natural for me to share it. I've learned that through service to others, we can transform ourselves and the world in which we live.

And, in case you're wondering, I safely made it off the pyramid. I came down on my butt clinging to the rope to start and trying not to pee my pants. About halfway down, I stood up and conquered each step with careful delight, even stopping for a photo op along the way with my girlfriends. It was flawless.

Chapter 3
THE DESTINY ROADMAP FRAMEWORK

Y ou know deep inside that it's time to move on, whether it's from a job that leaves you feeling broken, a soul-shattering relationship, or a dead-end town. You stay longer than is healthy, you look for reasons why it could work, and you ignore the numerous signs you've been given that it's time to let go. You're in the most painful part of The Void.

What's usually happening at this point is a period of discernment, withdrawal, and sensitivity. It's a period of mental suffering, as we're usually wrestling with ourselves over whether to stay or go. It's hard to feel confident in either choice since both have pros and cons associated with them; we exhaust the review from every angle. We shed more tears than we'd like to admit, but at some point, staying will become so uncomfortable that there is no choice but to push forward and release. You'll be thrust further into the place you're trying so hard to avoid, the emptiness and fear of the unknown.

Rather than feeling lost, you can put the steps in this book into action in your own life. You can begin to think of The Void as a blank chalkboard. This chalkboard is waiting for you to fill it with ideas, desires, and thoughts about where you were and where you'd like to be. It's waiting for you to get in touch, even though fear is typically running the show. That's where the steps come in.

Once you've made the decision to walk further into The Void, these are the essential elements you can practice that help you zero in and move past the resistance. These elements can help relieve the pressure and stress that usually ride along with fear in a sidecar.

These are the steps to learn how to co-create your Destiny Roadmap with the Universe and how to enjoy this time of exploration, discovery, and design in line with the plan in place for your life.

Step 1 – Acceptance

This step is about acknowledgment and acceptance for what we're leaving behind – no matter how relieved we might be to be out. It's the first step in setting the course toward something new, once we decide to move forward and close the door behind us.

Step 2 – Survey the Landscape

This step could also be called Pause. Surveying the landscape allows us to take stock of where we are. We can celebrate our freedom and explore our gifts, which helps us figure out where we're headed.

Step 3 – Direct your Drive

In this step, we discuss the importance of setting intentions and making commitments to ourselves. We could be here a while; might as well have fun and make some progress.

Step 4 – Flipping Stones

Now that we know our intentions and commitments, we can begin to explore how they resonate in our lives. We'll discuss various ways to take action and what it means to leave no stone unturned.

Step 5 – Forgiveness

We went through a lot before we decided to walk away. We may have some indents where a foot left an imprint. Forgiveness is not always easy to do when our subconscious wants to place blame for where we are. But the payoff is huge as we explore the release in this step.

Step 6 – Follow your Bliss

Many of us don't put ourselves first. In this step, we explore what we need in order to completely let go. What do we need to move forward as the person we're becoming on the journey of the Destiny Roadmap? This step is all about soul care and finding out what that means individually.

Step 7 – Mind the Mind

The mind is a crafty bugger. At this point we're ready to answer to the perpetual authority that lives in our heads in order to put its bullying and commentary to rest.

Step 8 – Invest in Yourself

This is where we pull it all together and reveal the secret of the entire Destiny Roadmap Framework. Hint: this is what we're doing all along as we follow the steps. It's a solid plan. I want to show you why it's ok to decide to step into the unknown and face your fears with courage. It's not as scary as it seems, I promise.

Chapter 4
STEP I: ACCEPTANCE

"To rid yourself of old patterns, focus all your energy not on struggling with the old, but on building the new."

DAN MILLMAN, *The Way of the Peaceful Warrior*

My sister criticizes me and points out everything wrong with me, from her perspective. She is a serious people pleaser and gets uncomfortable in situations where she feels like I might offend one of our clients. Then she gets angry and verbally attacks me.

When things don't go as planned, like I have in my head, I wonder why and realize that I'm assuming we're on the same page and then realize we aren't. We probably rarely have been. I feel it in my stomach. I feel angry and then depressed.

I'm tired of consistently compromising my well-being. I feel foolish, stupid and immature for not being more aware of this sooner.

I've fantasized about what to do from here, but I've been afraid to make any decisions, until now.

When my client, Athena, realized she was in The Void, it was like a light bulb switched on; she identified with it immediately, and she was relieved to learn it was possible to find a way out. When we first consciously arrive, it's disorienting, and we don't understand where we are. We have no idea what we're doing or who we are without the experience that defined our existence. What we do know is there was a pull, a magnetic force calling us to do something else, to be somewhere else, but we have no idea where or what that was. This is the Soul Calling. I tell clients that it's like the phone is ringing, and we don't know how to answer it. It's trying to reach us, to get our attention.

For a number of reasons, we ignore the call at first. We reason with ourselves about where we are. We push aside the signs and continue to live in a picture we paint of who we think we're supposed to be. That's where you are right now. I've been there too, a number of times.

Many times we're trying to do everything right, and in that, we end up doing everything wrong – *for ourselves.* We feel lost and fail to recognize who we've become. In my last experience, the one that brought me most recently into The Void, my confidence was rattled. I no longer showed up as my authentic self. I began hiding in plain view. It's as if the painful experience caused me to doubt myself and my decisions, in spite of my years of inner work. Even though I loved so many things about the job, I didn't love who I was in it, and that's what I had to accept before I could answer the call to walk away.

This is the first step in the journey to figure out where we're headed once we choose The Void completely. What we typically think is, *How can we jump right into acceptance? We've built a life around our career. Don't we need to go through some other steps before we can accept it?* Let's start with the third question, and in that answer we'll take care of the other two. Absolutely, yes, there are a bunch of stages we'll go through before we reach the Step of Acceptance in The Void, even before we walk away.

To understand where we are in relation to acceptance, I utilize a version of the Kübler-Ross model of the Five Stages of Grief. This model was first introduced back in 1969 in the book *On Death and Dying* by Elisabeth Kübler-Ross. Kübler-Ross's stages were inspired by her work with terminally ill patients.

The Kübler-Ross stages are Denial, Anger, Depression, Bargaining and Acceptance (DABDA). We don't have to experience each stage in the grief journey, we can skip stages as well as move back and forth between them. There is no right or wrong way to move through the process. The idea is we keep moving, processing, and feeling our way through it all and show up, in spite of the pain.

I first learned the steps in a cancer support group I joined after my mom died. There was a lot of sharing and listening in this group, but there was no one on the other side of grief, shining a light on where we could be. Grieving is a personal process, and in my process, I needed someone who was ahead of me lighting the path. I didn't want to stew in my own juices and keep going over how sad I was. Thankfully, I was in two programs concurrently, the other being AA. I saw a clear line where one program had a way out of the pain and the other didn't. AA program = solution. Stay sober; work the program, and you can find your way out. That's why the Destiny Roadmap Framework is comprised of actionable steps.

It took me five years to adjust to life without my mom - read that as *accept the change*. I moved in and out of the different stages over that time. After that experience, it became clear to me that we move in and out of these stages at other times in our lives as well, even during organizational change. I watched as employees went through some version of these steps when a change initiative was introduced that had some effect on how they did their jobs, even if we'd taken the time to gather input, invite them to meetings, produce memos, you name it. When the change happened there were people who would be shocked that it occurred, adamant the change wouldn't work, and resolute that we should return to our old ways. They had a hard time finding acceptance for the change, and so they remained stuck in pain of their own making, created by their thoughts about how the change was disrupting their life.

It's nearly impossible to move forward in The Void unless we've found acceptance for what we're leaving behind. In order to do that, I utilize a version of the DABDA model to help get us there. I call my version the Circle of Acceptance. These are the stages you'll typically go through to reach Acceptance in The Void. They look like this:

Good Times: *Everything is going along just fine. Life is pretty good. No useless roadblocks ahead.*

Realization: *Excuse me, why am I feeling so unsettled?! Why does it seem like everything is blowing up in my face? What the hell?*

Denial/Doubt: *This can't be happening, right? Everything was just dandy, wtf?*

Anger: *Screw this! This sucks!*

Bargaining/Confusion: *It's probably only temporary. I can fix this. Can't I? I can't! Oh, maybe I can.*

Sadness/Hurt/Self Pity: *I just want to crawl in a hole. It's not getting better. Someone please tell me what to do! I should've seen this coming. Now what?*

Alignment/Acceptance: *I don't see any other way. I'm scared to death, but I know I this isn't working anymore. I can't keep ignoring it.*

If you look at your current experience, you're probably in some sort of situation that has you transitioning in and out of the different stages above. Even the question, *Should I stay or should I go*, is a trigger. I know how distressing it is when we first realize our life might be calling for a change, and we resist the call. We may not even initially recognize it as a call. At some point, though, it becomes clear, and the more we resist, the more the pain amps up and our soul moves beyond calling to yelling. I've seen clients who've been pushing aside the knowledge that they needed to make a change for so long that, by the time they reach me, their pain is punching them in the gut.

Typically there are more than enough signs and warnings in the early stages of The Void, but we push them aside because we're scared – scared that we'll make the wrong decision and fearful that we're misinterpreting our instincts. We don't know where we're headed, so fear steps in to remind us we have no idea what our life will look like if we let go. We have a fear of walking away: fear of the unknown.

Built into these steps is a way to face our FEAR; I call it the FEAR Method. In it we agree to:

Face [it]

Embrace [it]

Accept [it]

Release [it]

(**S**hift – which comes later in the steps)

If we can find a way to turn fear into an ally, we're on our way toward releasing some of its power over us. It's not necessary for me to define fear for anyone in The Void. We each have a PhD in our own fear. We recognize it, we know how it cripples us, we know how it shows up, and we're more than aware of its ability to take over and initiate its hijacking agenda. Whether we break out in a sweat, have butt trembles, get nauseated, or feel concern, anxiety, panic or dread, there's no denying that when fear shows up, it immediately stops us in our tracks. It can be all-consuming.

There's a process of acceptance involved when fear shows up. 'Accept' is the "A" in the FEAR Method above, but there are steps in this method that precede acceptance. Those steps are **F**ace and **E**mbrace – and this is easier said than done. In the beginning it feels uncomfortable and awkward; we're on automatic for how we usually approach our fear and those reactions kick in. By agreeing to face and embrace our fears once we fully step into The Void, we start to reprogram those gut instincts to turn and run.

When we spend time practicing how to face our fears, our time in The Void becomes much easier. We'll have more clarity, and we can set ourselves up for success on the other side of The Void. Making the decision to let go is the hardest part. The next is being able to manage the fear.

Fear will tell us there is no other option than the one it's presenting. Usually what's on the docket is variations of flee; bolt; get the hell out; remove ourselves from the situation immediately. These are all outcomes that fear has decided are perfectly reasonable. Once fear takes hold, we convince ourselves that it's right, that the best way to get rid of the feeling is to retreat. The interesting thing is, we have the choice to act on what it's presenting by running away or turning and facing it head on, all of it, no matter how scary it feels.

In The Void, just like in other parts of life, fear is trying to protect us. It can be extremely helpful if we're walking down a trail and encounter a Pit Viper, but in The Void, we're just trying to figure out what to do, and fear is working hard to butt in. We don't have to accept the reality it's presenting. The only place fear resides is in our mind. It's not real, but since fear hijacks our emotional state, it's hard to believe that at first. I get it, but if we can simply agree to accept that fear is presenting us an alternate reality that it thinks we need to be aware of, we have a choice to *buy in* or not. The story isn't important, just the idea that fear is making a presentation for review, and we're going to take a moment to acknowledge and accept that, for ourselves and our fear – making it an ally. At that point, we can thank it for the information, release it (as best we can), and move forward. It's not always that simple, I know. It takes practice, because the physical reactions when fear moves in are strong, especially at first. But over time, and through diligent practice, we begin to be the commander of our own body responses to fear, rather than the other way around. I can't promise fear will completely go away – in fact, I can pretty much guarantee it won't – but the more we practice this process, the easier it becomes. Another way to look at this is: Fear resides in our mind, and comfort and confidence reside in our heart. We want to navigate The Void from our heart, rather than our mind. We'll dive further into this and the FEAR Method in Step 2.

The steps in The Void all work together to help us get past the surface emotions and go more deeply. That's where we can choose how to respond instead of being reactionary. We can recognize the difference between the fear of a situation that is not serving us and the fear of choosing to jump out of that airplane.

When clients first learn the FEAR Method, I remind them to be gentle, to think of it as new. *New* is just starting out. We're not expected to know everything, especially when we're beginners, and that can be a challenging feeling for many of us. When we apply the approach of **F**ace, **E**mbrace, **A**ccept, **R**elease, we have a tool to assist us in working with our fear. It reminds us there's another way other than giving in to the takeover.

I like to imagine fear as a little child tugging continuously on our coat with focused diligence on getting our attention. It can be incredibly annoying to have this little child yanking on our coat when we're trying to focus on something else, like our shortness of breath. At some point the child wins and gets our attention, and we either tell them to stop it and go away or we find the compassion in ourselves to give them the attention they're asking for.

When fear crops up in The Void, we imagine it as a little child who wants to tell us something they feel is incredibly important. Take the time to pause and listen to what it has to say, then decide where to go from there. Usually it just wants to be heard so we can say, *Thank you, I've considered the input*, and move forward or step back, depending on what we heard. As humans, it can be extremely challenging for us when we don't feel heard, so when our fear is showing up, we remember it wants to have a voice in the situation and the more we push it aside, the more desperately fear tries get our attention. So this step is all about accepting and acknowledging where we are when we arrive in The Void and also understanding that fear is going to try to insert itself whenever it can.

I know this about fear in The Void: It doesn't think we have a plan, but we do. Once we walk away, we know in our heart we can't go back to the way it was. The only way out of The Void is forward, so the plan is that we figure it out from here. It's a solid place to begin. We utilize the Destiny Roadmap Framework to figure out what our soul is calling for when we're grappling with the question of *should I stay or should I go*. It's where you are right now. Isn't it better to go forward and see what's here in The Void, even though you might be scared? To move through the Circle of Acceptance? Think about it, there have been numerous signs that you're no longer where you're meant to be. They were there for me too. Maybe it's felt deep in the gut like a sickening feeling – like when I would physically want to throw up when exiting the elevator at the Wall St. job. It might just randomly pop into our heads that it may be time for a change. It can even come in our dreams. I knew it was time to move from NYC when I was having dreams that I was pulling up the floorboards in my apartment and planting trees and flowers. That was a clear sign I needed to get out of the concrete maze and back to the land. My soul was speaking to me.

In the beginning, it's hard to connect with it, but once we commit to following these steps, they can help clear our mind and get us in touch. For now, in this step, we're only required to work on letting go, recognizing our fears, and finding acceptance for where we are.

A great way to do this is through journaling on specific questions like, *What did you learn about yourself in the experience that brought you into The Void?* or *What fears do you have about where you are now?*

Journaling can help you gain clarity about walking further into The Void. Remember, you're already in The Void; the decision has already been made. You know this somewhere deep inside, and journaling can help you connect with the calling, the voice inside that's telling you there is something more. Be sure to tune in to your heart.

I recommend spending 15 minutes a day writing in a journal, preferably in the morning. Ideally do this at the same time each day. The idea is to get whatever is in your head out onto paper and start clearing the landscape – which leads us to Step 2.

Through this step, we can start building a foundation for a deeper understanding of our true desires and our direction out of The Void. It's the beginning of creating our Destiny Roadmap.

Chapter 5

STEP 2: SURVEY THE LANDSCAPE

"I listen to my dreams and intuitions. When I do, things seem to fall into place. When I do not, something invariably goes awry."

DR. BRIAN L. WEISS, *Many Lives, Many Masters*

When clients begin this step, they write out any advice they can give themselves about where they are at this moment in time, because this step is about a pause in the moment to reflect.

Tina: *Relax. Be curious about the journey. A process is in motion. There has definitely been progress. Remember to breathe, to focus on the breath, over and over again. Practice. Enjoy where I am right now.*

Brandi: *Don't feel guilty. Move forward with intention. Love yourself. I am enough. Trust the process. Everything I need is inside of me. Take your time. Be quiet and listen.*

Our minds can be on the 100 other things we feel we should be doing in any given situation, even in The Void. We don't often stop and take a breath.

In Step Two, we survey the landscape, which means we take stock of where we are, both inside and out. The way we do that is by taking a moment to hit the pause button, and in that pause, we get out of the maze and get in touch with where we are. Instead of rushing from point A straight to point B in The Void, we look at what's in between. There's work involved here. We're not just sitting around drinking Thai Basil Margaritas, although if you need one, please partake – they're yummy, and you've been through a lot.

This step encompasses a bit of exploration, assessment, and consideration. We land on unfamiliar ground in The Void. Instinctively, we have the idea that we better get our butt in gear so we can figure out what the hell we're doing from here.

What's behind the *get going* thought is fear. Fear of not having security, a job, money coming in, a lack of direction, loneliness, of judgment from others, of loss of our previous life, fear of what to do next; you name it, fear owns it. The biggest fear of all? Fear of the unknown. It's a lot to process, and our fear creates confusion at this point, so we press the pause button and take a moment to get in touch, discover our surroundings, and turn a light on, so to speak, since it's a little dark when we arrive in The Void.

The thought of hitting pause can bring up stress. Stress is simply the body's response to external stimuli. The external stimuli bring fear to the forefront so we can get a good look at it. When we stop and look at what causes the stress, the stimuli become eye openers; something that pushes and motivates us to pay attention. When we're surveying the landscape, our fear is there to encourage us to listen up, wake up, regroup, and redefine ourselves in The Void. If we don't come to terms with the reality that a pause is necessary and we march ahead down the same path we just left, something will happen to make sure we get the message that we left that path for a reason. I've seen it many times in my own life and in the lives of my clients.

Brandi worked more than 20 years in management. Her most recent job, the experience that brought her into The Void, had been fulfilling, but very stressful. When she finally made the decision to let go and walk away, she had spent a good year waffling between anger and sadness in the Circle of Acceptance, with a moment or two of confusion and bargaining thrown in for good measure. Initially, she applied for what seemed like a perfect job in her field. She was highly recommended and had two great interviews. She was surprised when they called to tell her they liked her, but they had gone with someone else for the position. Her ego was a little bruised, but she figured it was meant to be and spent time with her family.

A month or so later, she applied for a position with another company. She had two more excellent interviews, but again they called to say they had gone with another person, even though they liked her and she was more than qualified.

When she was turned down for the third position that was perfect for her in six months, she came to me in disbelief. Brandi was a big fish in a small pond. The companies would have been lucky to have her skill set and experience. I understood why she was floored when she received the call that they had also gone with someone else. It was hard for her to see beyond the disbelief, but when I met with her it was clear to me she was being called to do something different; she just couldn't see it. It was easier to think she could just get another well-paying job in her familiar and comfortable profession.

When I asked her how she would have felt if she'd gotten the third job, she was resigned. I asked her what it felt like when she was walking into the building for the interview. I wanted her to describe not only her feelings about the people and the job, but the physical landscape as well. As she began talking, it became clear to her she didn't want to work there: *My heart isn't in it. It would be going backwards. I'd be settling. I'm not even a little excited about it. What I am excited about is the idea that I could've made a comparable salary to the one I just left.* That was not feeding her soul, it was appeasing her fear.

Once she came to that conclusion, she was ready to stop applying for any more management positions. Her career had served her well for many years, but it was time to figure out if she was meant to head in a new direction. She began to imagine what she could be doing, she understood this was her opportunity to build a new fire out of the ashes. About three weeks into our work together, she realized she needed that third company to tell her that she was going in a different direction. It wasn't easy for her to see at first, even though everything was pointing that way.

Part of this step involves finding your footing after a long period of tripping and picking yourself up again. We spend a fair amount of time in the *should I stay or should I go* phase, which hurts. We have permission to take a moment and let the fog clear. Fog doesn't just create a lack of vision, it can leave behind a layer of dripping moisture, weighing heavily on the trees and grass. This goes away when the sun comes out and the air warms up. Surveying the landscape allows time for the sun to come out and light our surroundings. It's about finding ourselves and reconnecting after a long hiatus. We're in the process of self-discovery after coming further into The Void, and this reconnection is like running into our favorite person we haven't seen for a long time. Our heart opens, and we instantly reach out to embrace them. We want to catch up on everything we've missed. Their voice is a warm caress we've been searching for without knowing it.

This step is about taking inventory of our situation to date, by checking in with ourselves.

We take the time to look back so we understand that even though we're thrilled to be out of the weight of the experience, there were some amazing gifts we received during that time. It wasn't all bad, or we wouldn't have tried to make it work for so long. We honor what we left behind. We learned a lot and it served a purpose, even though it may feel like the only purpose was to piss us off. There's more, I promise. We have to be open to the learning so we can move through the lesson and let go of what we thought *would* be in order to experience what's *meant* to be.

A day after I climbed the pyramid in Coba, I sat down in my room in Tulum, and I wrote a list of 25 gifts my experience had given me. It wasn't easy, because I was still hurt, but it shifted my perspective toward a more positive outlook. I ask clients to do the same thing, and then we utilize the list throughout the steps to help release and pivot. We make a bullet list – no stories necessary, since we know what each one means. We write down 25, even if we have to work for it. There are gifts to be found if we're open to looking.

We examine the gifts from the past, and consider how they might serve us in The Void and beyond. When we can make the connection that something positive came out of our situation, we're closer to moving forward.

I'm a firm believer in finding the silver lining and looking at what we learn in any given situation, no matter how challenging it might be. There are lessons in everything when we take the time to look and listen, even if the lesson is, *I don't want to do that again!*

An important part of this step involves seeking answers to why something happened. We look to create meaning for ourselves so we can move on and find closure. Sometimes we can't figure out the why until we're on the other side of it, or maybe even later in life. We have a narrow vantage point, where we are on our life journey, that can cause us to feel limited in our scope, but we're not as limited as we think. Many people feel like life is working against them, but in reality, life is working in our favor more than we know, and this will become clearer as we move through the steps.

We feel more secure with looking outside ourselves for answers, and we're trained to listen to our mind. We're trained to allow our mind to convince us of a number of things, just like when our fear is convincing us of our limitations. Our mind believes it's receiving As in the lessons of our life, but it has a way of distorting our perspective at times.

I had a client who spent a lot of time buying into her self-doubt and resistance. I told her she wanted to focus her work on getting out of her head. She asked me, *If I'm not in my head, where am I?* This isn't a crazy question. We spend so much time in our heads, the idea of being somewhere else is initially foreign. We don't even know where that other place is. When I told her it was her heart, she was silent for a moment, and then she softly asked, *How do I do that?* Well, it takes practice and time to bust through the protective walls we build around our hearts. Typically, we're not in touch with what our heart wants;

we trudge through life with our heads leading the way. When we learn how to drop into our heart and figure out what it wants, it can be life-changing. I literally cried happy tears.

Once you connect, you never want to be disconnected again. It's a daily practice, at first, since it feels unnatural and it can take some time to get used to, but it's worth every second of the time put in. Think about this: Where does your mind doubt what your heart already knows? If you can come up with even one example, you're in touch with your heart, and that's a start. It may even provide the spark you need to fully make the leap into The Void.

We're discussing the heart, because we utilize it as a way to move forward in The Void and connect with where we're being led. Whatever the experience is, there's no doubt it's painful, but it's likely there will be a deeper meaning to discover. It's usually not what we think we're doing when we walk away. It's why my client Brandi applied for three more jobs in her field of expertise. She thought she walked away from her situation for one reason, when in reality she left because she was meant to be doing something more aligned with her soul and her heart's desire, something that caused her less stress, less sadness, and less struggle. Not that her old profession didn't align with her heart. It did for a long time.

We grow and evolve through our experiences, so it's only natural that we'll outgrow careers and evolve into new ones. We don't often speak about this, because many people spend a lot of time trying to fit their growing self into their old life. For a number of reasons, it's difficult to fully walk away. The main reason is fear. But when the calling is so deep, the Universe will step in to ensure we make the shift. It's happening *for* you, not *to* you – just as my coach said to me when I was waffling between *should I stay or should I go*. Maybe this is where you are as well? Is your experience happening for you?

In a sense, this step of Survey the Landscape is the bridge from *what was* to *what's meant to be*. It's the heart of The Void, which can make this step challenging for some. It can be difficult because we turn the focus on ourselves, something most of us have spent little time doing in our experience.

As part of this step we listen and explore, with curiosity. When we take time to listen, we begin to hear the call more clearly. It is that same call that's making itself known in the Circle of Acceptance. The call that can take a while to get through, because we're busy trying to figure out how to fix *where* we are rather than working on listening to *who* we are and who we want to be. So we listen now.

During my year in The Void, I recognized the need to gain more perspective and clarity. I knew I wanted to get in touch more deeply, and one way I knew to do that was to have an Akashic Records reading.

I've known about the Akashic Records for years, ever since I was sitting on the floor of Barnes and Noble devouring spiritual books. At one point, I came across Edgar Cayce who referred to the Akashic Records as the Book of Life or the Universe's super-computer system. Cayce first introduced me to the idea of an energetic place we could access that stored our soul's past lives, experiences, gifts, life lessons, and so much more.

In Chapter 4, I told you I was interested in metaphysics when I was younger, but there wasn't anyone in my life who could help me explore my curiosity, so I went through my teens hiding the fact that I always felt like I knew more than I should about situations and people. At my college graduation, I was having a conversation with my dad and he mentioned that my Nana got his family through the Depression by doing readings for people. I was shocked and relieved all at the same time. It somehow gave me validation for everything I'd felt growing up.

In that instant, I knew deep inside me I also wanted to do readings for people, but I had no idea how, and I put it all on the back burner for years, until my spiritual awakening in AA.

When I read about the Akashic Records, somewhere inside me I knew them to be the truth and an extremely powerful resource. I'd attempted to access the records a number of times to connect to my energetic soul profile and my past lives, but it was slow going, and the connection wasn't strong. Once I was in The Void, I knew the information could help me gain clarity, so I had a reading done in order to expedite the process.

In truth, I wanted to be able to access my own records, but I was also testing the water for the possibility of learning how to access the records for other people. Before I walked away from my job, my coach said, *If you could do anything you wanted, what would you do?* Out of my mouth tumbled, *I'd do readings.* Of course she wasn't expecting to hear that answer. *Like psychic readings?* It was one of only a handful of times that I'd said it out loud. *Why don't you?* she asked. It was such a simple question, but one I hadn't actually considered for years. It seemed so distant from who I was in my career. When she proposed it, my heart skipped a beat in the best way possible. I was excited to consider it.

During my Akashic Records reading, I saw the path I could take to put the information to use going forward and apply it to create the life I'd always desired. It also confirmed that I wanted to read the Akashic Records for other people. The information contained in the records is incredibly validating and useful, so I became certified in reading the records.

Once I started doing readings for people from all over the world, I could see the difference it made in their lives. Clients had more confidence and clarity about where they were, but a few wanted to know what more they could do with the information, and I found myself coaching beyond the readings. It took me decades to give myself the opportunity to do something I'd always wanted to do. Once I was in The Void and doing it all differently, I realized I needed to stop denying that part of myself and stop worrying about what other people would think; I haven't looked back. Is there something you're denying in yourself? What have you always wanted to do, but have never given yourself the opportunity to try? If you aren't sure, it's ok. We'll learn how to discover that through the steps.

The Destiny Roadmap utilizes, in part, specific information from a client's Akashic Records. During a reading, I gather key aspects that we use to help create a map for their current life, where they've been and where they are now – and we apply it to their path forward. It offers clients clarity, direction, and tools to face their fears with courage and begin to work with the Universe to co-create the life of their dreams, a life they're excited about.

This is exactly what I did for myself to follow my heart and not let my fear take over and lead the way. I put my trust in the Universe and co-created a life I love, in line with my Destiny Roadmap.

We want to understand our lives and experiences – give them meaning. When we reconnect with ourselves and our past in this way, it has the power to shift our perspective enough to see that we're experiencing our lives in a way that has an underlying purpose. We're calling experiences to us so we can continue to learn, so we can get on the path that best aligns with our heart and soul. But we may not see it if we don't take the time to pause. And this is where the adventure begins, once we make the decision to let go in The Void.

Chapter 6
STEP 3: DIRECT YOUR DRIVE

What the caterpillar calls the end of the world,
the master calls a butterfly."

RICHARD BACH, *Illusions*

When my client Tina finished Step 2, she felt excited, like the horizon seemed hazy and unknown, but she felt a new reality being born. It was still mysterious. She said, *the mystery makes me feel alive, like I'm in a period of creation and potential. It feels like waking up and reinvention.* For the first time in years, her instincts were firing on all cylinders. Perfect for this next step as we switch gears to *Direct Your Drive*.

In this step we begin the process to connect the dots and identify our true calling. Drive is about energy, determination, and motivation: everything this step encompasses. Here's where we apply what we've learned so far to propel ourselves forward in The Void. We do this by setting intentions and making commitments.

There's comfort in this step, because we're finally taking action toward finding the door out of The Void.

We aren't done with Steps 1 and 2, but we do keep moving forward, even though we may swing back and forth at times. So while we're setting intentions and making commitments, we may still be working on Acceptance about what happened and where we are. Most definitely we'll be utilizing the FEAR Method to address our fear as it comes up. Don't forget that we're also putting the information from the Akashic Records reading to good use. All of this is laying the groundwork for the road ahead.

So what's the difference between an intention and a commitment, and why aren't we using the term "goals" here?

Intentions are a plan with a purpose. There's a target and a motivation for what and why, but not always for how. That's the secret in this step, and it can be life-changing. It's what I was talking about in the moment when I realized the answer to my philosophical uncertainty was AA, even though it seemed strange at the time. I didn't question the *how* of AA; I just decided to embrace the *what* and see where it led. This is where we begin to partner with the Universe and co-create the life we desire.

The best news is, we don't have to decide on one specific intention. We can have the cake and eat it too – and we'll still fit in those jeans, so to speak. Remember those jeans that were two sizes too small? In this step, they start to feel a little more comfortable, because the work is about the connection to our heart and soul. We haven't necessarily lost any physical weight. What we're losing is emotional weight, which can help us *feel* lighter energetically. When we allow ourselves to work from this place, we have more clarity about our path; we begin to understand why we want what we want and take steps to create it. The amazing thing is, once we decide on the aligned *what*, the Universe begins creating it on the other side for us. It's the door out of The Void, and the path begins to illuminate as we peel away the layers to reach our core, the heart.

Commitments are a pledge or a promise we make to ourselves about a certain undertaking we feel it's important to pursue. It's a vow we make to ourselves that we're going to work to fulfill, no matter what obstacles or challenges appear in our path. In essence, we're making a commitment here to show up for ourselves and our intentions. There's no use setting intentions if we aren't planning on seeing them through, so the commitments are exactly about that. Through our commitments we're saying, *I will do this no matter what gets in the way. I spent time narrowing it down, and now I'm ready to roll.*

There isn't anyone in The Void saying we can't do this or do that. That can be empowering and frightening all at the same time. My friend and mentor, Peggy, often told me, *It's time to take your emergency brake off.* I often did, but fear was always right behind me, ready to jump in uninvited. I spent so many years afraid to discover what I truly wanted, afraid to reveal what was inside, wondering if what I had to say really mattered. Could it make a difference? I was living in the back seat, and fear was driving. It wasn't until I'd done the work to get below the layers of fear and anxiety that I began to find the way out. I grew stronger, but there was still a little fortress around my heart. Trust was huge for me, and it took time to break through that barrier and let people in. It took even longer to let myself out; to allow myself to open up to who I truly was. Every time I heard someone say it was time for me to step into my power, I wanted to throw up. *What the hell did that mean, and where was I supposed to be stepping when I felt surrounded by land mines?* In those moments it's all about trusting the path.

Setting intentions and making commitments is about the exact same thing. It takes trust, a trust that we may not have fully developed yet, but we're creating that trust through the steps in The Void and through the co-creation of the Destiny Roadmap. The relationship grows stronger with the desire to progress through The Void by setting intentions, even though we aren't quite sure how they'll materialize.

So why am I staying away from *goals*? Goals are focused on a result. Think about it in sports where the players are focused on the outcome of winning the game. Goals, like a sports game, have a fixed timeframe that can create pressure when applied to our own lives. If we don't achieve our goal in the set amount of time, we can get down on ourselves for missing it. Many times we set goals for things we don't enjoy doing– losing weight, exercising, or saving money, so we set ourselves up for failure from the start. Goals can help us feel like we're headed somewhere, but they can also take the enjoyment out of the process of getting there. We can be so focused on the result that we miss the journey to the result. In short, goals can feel constricting, and we don't want to constrict anything in The Void. We want to feel free and open to create.

In business, we often discuss SMART goals: Specific, Measurable, Achievable, Relevant, and Timed for an outcome. Goals in business are important to keep the organization on track and moving forward as a whole, with everyone focused on the same goals for a specified amount of time, e.g., a fiscal year. That's a good thing. We don't use goals in The Void, because we don't want to place limitations on ourselves for what's possible. Yes, we will be specific, in a way, but we're not really measuring anything, and we're definitely not looking at what we feel is achievable in the sense that we choose intentions that we know we can attain, so we feel better about ourselves in the end. We're setting heart-centered intentions, things that make our soul feel wildly alive. We aren't concerned with *when* they'll be achieved; we're not even concerned with *how* they'll be achieved. We're playing with the idea that our future is limitless. We just want to know *what* we'd like to achieve.

In order to set intentions and commitments, clients consider the discoveries from the previous steps of Acceptance and Survey the Landscape. When we combine that with the Akashic Records information, it's the beginning of a powerful roadmap. I encourage clients to make some choices that are outside of whatever they think it is they *should* be doing. To think about what might make them feel fulfilled, not what they think will bring them money or even security. *What have they always wanted to do? What would their dream life look like? Describe a perfect day.* These are all questions that can get us thinking about some intentions. I set the intention that I was going to do readings for people. I didn't worry about the how. I just wrote it down.

When I first met my client Elijah, he was in deep pain and confusion about where he was. He'd been in The Void for more than a year. He'd taken some steps to try to feel better, even walking away from his situation into a new life and scene, but he felt lost about his direction. At 50, he was feeling pressured to find something to do that would generate enough money for retirement. He wanted to be of service, but he was more concerned with security. He could see a self imposed horizon and felt desperate to figure out what would help him feel stable before he got there. He had three very different ideas when we sat down together, but none of them connected deeply with his heart and soul.

During our conversation, I asked him which one he'd choose if money wasn't a factor. He said he'd choose a job that involved travel, because it was more freeing. He described to me a younger version of himself at 31. He was animated, and he came alive when he connected to his heart and to the young, free-spirited person who landed in a new place with bright eyes and a quest for experience, someone who didn't have the horizon in his sight. This was not the person who was sitting in front of me. This person was allowing fear to lead him, not understanding why it wasn't taking him to a place of happiness. He was searching for something, but he had no idea what.

I asked him, *is your 31-year old, free-spirited self here now?* His shoulders dropped and tears welled up in his eyes as he connected to the truth when he answered with a heartfelt, *No, he's not.*

We discussed the idea of making fulfilling choices in The Void, even though we're scared. That we have the freedom to rediscover and reconnect with ourselves, and once we do, we can find the way out.

When we're setting intentions and making commitments, we do our best to connect to that part of ourselves that is on this journey for the experience, the one who knows we were led into The Void for a reason. Why not throw caution aside and be bold by choosing something because it feels good rather than right? There are certain things we thrive on, that make our heart sing; we need to make sure we include those here. Are you feeling like you're ready to step into The Void completely? If you did, what intentions might you set that include your dreams? The things that are going to make you feel fulfilled? It's important to connect with your heart. What intentions could you set and what commitments could you make to help you see those intentions through? I know you're still lurking here, but it's ok to try this out and see how it feels. All we're required to do in this step is set some intentions and make some commitments. It doesn't come from the outside. It comes from the inside. We decide we're going to show up for ourselves in this new way, based on our intentions and commitments, and see what happens. Why don't you give it a try, and see how it feels?

I don't want to gloss over the FEAR that may have popped up just now. I get it. It can feel a little like we do something and then wait and see. It doesn't feel like we're doing anything at all. But we are. We're identifying where we want to put our energy going forward. It will be easier than we think, in fact. Whatever your mind is saying, just get out of there right now.

Before I went to Tulum, I set a clear intention about finding clarity on a decision. One of the *big* questions I had was whether or not I wanted to enter into a business opportunity with a friend. I had only walked away from my job two months before, and I didn't know if I wanted to jump into something right away, but I remained open to receiving an answer. I had no idea how the answer would come, but I trusted that I'd be able to make a decision when I returned. This is how we set our intentions, with the idea that we're open to the guidance and the direction the intention takes us. It's like having blind faith; we're putting our faith in the idea that we'll be guided. It takes a little bit of patience and a whole lot of trust.

I've been where you are. You know for a fact there's something inside of you saying, *It's time to move on; this is no longer aligning with my soul.* The calling was there for me too, but it can take time to be ready to answer. It's ok. Honestly, we all do it. At some point, we get in our own way and have doubts about the signs or our gut instincts. When we're fearful to make a change, we can sabotage ourselves. Stay with me, and we can find the inspiration you need to finally decide.

The important bit to hold onto here is directing our drive. This is all about getting clear on the general direction in which we want to head. That clarity doesn't come from the outside, it comes from the inside. We're not sitting down with an atlas to find the fastest route to Mexico. We're going inside to review everything we've done so far, put it all together, and make some choices about where to go from here. It's not a life sentence, and we can change our mind. For now, we just trust that we're making the right decisions and that we're being guided. It's all a practice, and when we put our faith in a practice even if it feels like it's still evolving, we strengthen our relationship with the unknown. That's one of the main reasons we're here: to strengthen that relationship and become more comfortable with ourselves, The Void, and the Universe.

By setting intentions and making commitments, we can make some progress. But in reality, every single thing we do in The Void is progress; so that's the best news of all.

Chapter 7
STEP 4: FLIPPING STONES

"Every moment of your life is infinitely creative and the universe is endlessly bountiful. Just put forth a clear enough request, and everything your heart truly desires must come to you."

SHAKTI GAWAIN, *Creative Visualization*

Once we spend time setting intentions and making commitments, there's a strong possibility that doubts will come up – *read that as fears*. So at this point, we take note of how we're managing our FEAR and utilizing the FEAR Method.

Previously, we discussed that when stress arises, it's just an indicator that we need to pay attention to the external stimuli that's initiating the stress. When resistance arises, it's another clue to pay attention to *why* we're resisting. Not surprisingly the resistance can be fear-based. One of my intentions is to not let fear run my life. I'm committed to facing my fears with courage. I check in using the FEAR method, and I do everything I can to move forward even when I'm scared. I *persist.* I have a saying for clients at this point: *When we resist, persist,* because there's typically a message behind the resistance

The resistance we faced in the last chapter, when we were setting intentions and making commitments, probably went something like this: *Who am I to think I can create something wildly amazing for my life? What if I'm not successful? What the hell am I doing?* That's a whole lot of doubt, insecurity, and reluctance happening, and what's typically underlying all of it is fear.

My client Brandi had the same fears when she started working on the intentions and commitments. She decided she wanted to start her own business, so she set the intention and committed to moving it forward in Step 3, but she immediately began to doubt her abilities once she wrote it down.

She would ask herself, *Are you really going to do this? What makes you think you can do this? You're making a huge blind step into entrepreneurism. but you have always been comfortable working for other people. Will people want to hire you?* Her mind was definitely interfering with her confidence. When it came up, she quickly recognized it and didn't let it take over. She engaged the FEAR Method and said to the little fearful Brandi tugging on her coat, *I hear you. I understand why you're scared, but it is going to be ok. I'm following my heart, and I will be safe and taken care of.* She could then reset and move forward. In our session she said, *Honestly, taking action, even when in fear, is so helpful rather than resisting and trying to ignore it.*

Remember, we want to invite fear to be a partner in our lives, a friend rather than an enemy. The idea of fear pulling on our coat works well, because we view our fear with compassion, like a little child. In Brandi's case, she imagines it to be her inner child who is fearful and needs to be heard.

We can utilize the FEAR Method to help us in any circumstance. When we feel fear come up, we **F**ace it (pause and deep breath), **E**mbrace it (check in and listen), **A**ccept it (acknowledge – without labels), **R**elease it (tell it, *I got this; it's ok*) – this all causes a **S**hift, so I add on an "s" to FEAR(S) since the entire method is all about shifting from where we are to where we want to be, in a place where fear hasn't emotionally hijacked us. So we **F**ace, **E**mbrace, **A**ccept, **R**elease and **S**hift. We decide to keep moving forward, even though fear is sitting right beside us. This brings us to Step 4 – Flipping Stones.

This step is where the rubber meets the road, and we buckle in and get moving on the intentions and commitments we set in the last step. This step can be fun if we hook into the idea that we're on a hunt for alignment and where we feel an intention resonate. An important part of this step is really understanding *what* we're doing. First, we're checking our intentions for positioning within our future life. How do we do that? By taking action, being open, and saying *yes,* even if everything inside us is saying, *I'm scared.* This is about co-creating with the Universe, exploration, and deciding where to take action. We're acting on the 'attractions' hidden in the intentions and commitments, and we examine how it feels to consider them. Why are we attracted to these particular intentions? We find out in this step by internally feeling the resonance and excitement for how our actions unfold. That excitement is a sign to persist, even if we feel the desire to resist at first and even if we want to hide.

At first this step can feel a little like we've arrived in a foreign country late at night, and we don't speak the language. We get in a cab and say, *Hi, please take me to this hotel.* We trust the driver to get us there, right? Usually, yes, but if fear is in charge, we start doubting and questioning everything. We start freaking out. Meanwhile, the driver is doing his thing, and he arrives at the destination. We realize the insane mental journey we just went on during the ride from the airport to the hotel. We worried the entire time when there was no need. We don't want to do that in this step. Taking action in this step is like telling the cab driver where we're going and trusting him to get there even though *we* don't know the way. He does. It's his job, but we have to take action and tell him where to go. He can't possibly get us to the destination if we don't tell him where it is. The Universe is the driver, and we're in the cab trusting that it knows exactly where it's taking us, because it has instructions on where we're headed. The Universe immediately sets a course to make it happen. It's like a spiritual GPS is set to get us from Point A (where we are) to Point B (where we want to be). We're in a reliable vehicle, we have a good cab driver so we can trust that we're going to get there even though we may not know exactly how, and we can even enjoy the ride along the way.

As we learn to stay connected with our heart and travel along our path, the map appears as we take each step on the journey. This is the Destiny Roadmap. The task in this step is to follow the map with trust that it's leading somewhere, a place in line with the discoveries we've made in The Void. A place that may surprise us along the way, so we remain open to how it unfolds.

My client Athena said, *I always thought of my life as my mind, my body, my spirit, but never included my heart in there. When I set my intentions, I was really looking at how I could come up with something that would put my heart out there to be acknowledged.* We keep that connection going while trying to decide on pursuits in line with our intentions and commitments. We want to remain open to anything, as The Void is limitless. The mind creates limits for us. That's why we stay connected to the heart, even if we keep bringing ourselves back to it again and again. We need to stay out of our heads.

Were you just in there? Don't worry, we're going to address that in Chapter 10, because it's important. But right now we're focused on our heart connection.

There's a little secret in this step. The Void can actually be a place of freedom rather than a place of fear. Freedom to be who we were born to be. Freedom to express ourselves in ways we never thought possible through our chosen life path. Freedom to do whatever lights us up – and it isn't all or nothing. It doesn't have to be one thing over the other. You don't have to completely give up everything that was working. It may just require a retooling. That's typically a relief for clients, because there are good things in what we leave behind. We discover this in our list of 25 gifts. This is how we utilize that list and put its contents toward co-creating a way out of The Void.

Freedom can feel paralyzing and uncomfortable, because there are limitless possibilities. and fear will typically rise up and try to insert itself. It can mean so many things: liberty, independence, lack of restraint, readiness, nonconformity; we don't have to define it completely now. Just know this is where we get going and have some fun in The Void.

This step is all about lack of restrictions, full play, and adventure. We delve into the intentions we set, and we do it with curiosity. We ask curious questions, explore with wonder, and receive answers with interest. In The Void, curiosity is about accepting the adventure while not having a tie to what it should look like; in other words, being open to the experience and what comes. There's a little bit of research and assessment here, but for the most part the exploration is about receiving with your heart and determining if it's worthy of further action. The curiosity allows for a level of consideration that keeps us in a place where we dig until we land on something that jives, that feels in alignment. Often, *we just know*.

This can show up in a number of ways, like a quote on our Instagram feed, or a song that's stuck in our heads and that perfect lyric line is the answer for the question we had the entire day before. It can even show up in a Google search list; one link may stand out over all the others. The answers start coming, the direction is revealed, and we go with it by following our heart, because we're relying on ourselves and our ability to receive, with curiosity, everything we need in any given moment. The curiosity allows us to explore freely, with wonder – *I wonder what this is about? I wonder where this will lead?* It doesn't feel like a life commitment when we ask this way.

And then, we receive the answers *with interest*. This is one of the best hacks I have for myself. With practice, I work hard to receive much of the information in my life with interest. *Hmmm, that's interesting,* or, *Isn't that interesting* has become a life saver. This tiny sentence is the one big strategy I have for not immediately labeling something good or bad. It works for so many things. In a conversation I may not agree with, it gives me time to disengage and remind myself to listen with curiosity. I don't have to pick a side; it doesn't have to affect the way I feel; it's just *interesting*. In this step, the information is allowed to come in without judgment from the mind. It puts a *comma* in the sentence of receiving rather than a *period*, because our mind wants to label it as *something* – usually good or bad, but not here in The Void (and perhaps not even in the rest of life). It's just interesting.

In the last chapter I told you I set an intention, before I left for Tulum, to receive an answer to whether or not I wanted to go into business with a friend when I returned. I had all kinds of questions about it. I knew the business well, since it was a small market in my community, but I wasn't clear about my involvement at first. There were a lot of pros and cons.

I wanted to help my friend; together, we made a great team. I wanted the market to remain in my small community, and I knew I had the skills to make it work. I even had a vision for what it could be; six years earlier when my husband and I were passing through the area on a scouting trip, we had lunch at that very market and talked with the owner. The place had so much potential, but there were no indoor bathrooms, and it was dark and needed a major remodel. Yet something was shining beneath the surface. About a mile down the road after we left, I said to my husband, *If I could get my hands on that place, it could be amazing.* End of story. That was it. I didn't even know my friend at the time, and I didn't even live in the state, let alone the community. When it presented itself years later, I couldn't get that out of my head. Even so, I was truly unclear about the decision.

I got my answer when I arrived on top of the pyramid in Coba. I spent a good hour up there, hanging out, taking pictures, and not getting close to the edge – I wasn't cured of my fear of heights, after all. At one point, there was a sense of knowing exactly what I was supposed to do. Yes, I would go into business with my friend, and I felt good about it. I received the answer when my heart was the most open it'd ever been in my life. I knew I would let nothing get in the way of the decision – not doubt, fear, worry, or concerns – I was clear that all those thoughts come from the mind rather than the heart, and I committed to stick with my heart decision, no matter what. That's the intention I set and the commitment I made.

Intention – purchase the business

Commitment – follow through and not let my mind take me into fear as we move forward. Remain in my heart.

I had no idea how it would unfold or how it would work out, I just kept moving forward and following the path. There have been some challenges and yes, some fears did pop up, mostly around personal finances, but the benefits and growth have far outweighed anything that arose. What I do know is it's allowed me to keep some parts of the former career I enjoyed, like ordering, customer service, baking, and being an active part of my community. I didn't have to give them up.

We can make our way through The Void with trust that we're being led, that it will work out, and that we don't have to choose one thing. I knew I'd have time to get the business up and running while I also put efforts into all the other things I felt called to do, like Akashic Records readings and writing a book.

When I said yes and set the intention to own the business, I felt confident that it didn't have to be one thing over the other. It could be one thing and all the others, if I chose, because going into business with my friend wasn't the only dream I had after walking into The Void, reconnecting with my truth, and creating my Destiny Roadmap.

My personal exploration in this step included reading books that called to me, visiting websites, watching webinars, and putting myself out there. I had tea with people I met through mutual friends, so I could pick their brain. I joined an accountability group, and I was open to the experience of being in The Void. It pushed me out of my comfort zone many times, and each time I checked in with my heart to gain clarity on where I was.

I searched for people who were where I wanted to be, for people who I'd like to work with or who were offering programs I could participate in to further my commitments. When something felt right and in alignment, I wasn't worried. I was excited to get started, which resonated for me, and I held onto that. I considered things that I didn't follow through on. It took that deep heart connection to figure out if it was the way forward or not. I took the time to go down the road, because sometimes it's just as important to figure out what we *don't* want so we recognize when we land on what we *do*.

Hopefully you're getting the picture here: The idea in this step is to leave no stone unturned. My husband Joe is the best at this. He literally flips stones over and checks out what's underneath. He's looking for insects, snakes, lizards... he's a nature guy. He wants to see what's hiding out in the places people don't normally think to look, because the creatures are resting safely. It's a great metaphor for this step. We want to find what's hiding within and around us, in places we don't normally think to look, like under a stone. Where can we look that we wouldn't normally think to seek direction at this point? It may not immediately occur to us where the best answers may come from, like at the top of a pyramid in the Yucatan or by picking the brain of someone we just met. When we remain open to how it all unfolds and we agree to say yes or maybe, rather than no, it starts to present in a way that makes sense, and we begin to connect the dots. The light gets brighter on our path, and our confidence builds because we're strengthening the trust in ourselves and our internal guidance by facing our fears a little bit at a time.

Chapter 8
STEP 5:
FORGIVENESS

"I never knew how strong I was until I had to forgive someone who wasn't sorry and accept an apology I didn't receive."

UNKNOWN

The familiar, soothing voice of Tamara Levitt, from the "Calm" meditation app I liked to listen to, echoed once again through my head. *Welcome to this 10-minute meditation on loving kindness.* As soon as she said that, I felt the knot in my throat. I felt the aching pain of the longing for forgiveness, forgiveness I'd been unable to conjure over the last few months of being in The Void. No matter how many times I'd pleaded with myself to develop feelings of warmth, compassion, and love toward myself and others, I had failed miserably.

It'd been months since I walked away from my job into The Void and closed the door behind me, yet I'd occasionally find myself in a confusing labyrinth of heartbreak. Midway through the

75

guided meditation came the suggestion yet again: *Now bring to mind an image of someone who has hurt you in the past... as best as you can, open your heart, if it's possible.* It wasn't hard for me to picture the people Tamara was talking about. What was hard was when she continued with: *And extend loving kindness to them by saying, may you be happy; may you be safe; may you be healthy; may you be at peace.* Ugh! Why was that so hard? Why couldn't I let it go? Why did I provide the space in my mind for the pain to continually wander through? I had to answer those questions for myself.

There's a strong possibility that whatever brings us into The Void might need a bit of reflection, soul searching, and perhaps even forgiveness. We forgive so we can let go of the past and have clarity and openness for what's ahead, after we walk out of The Void. Forgiveness is about understanding, so in this step we take a moment to figure out if we're hurt, bummed, sulky, or angry in some way. We even identify who or what might be the *object* of our irritation.

Forgiveness is important in The Void. The anger, animosity, or annoyances we hold onto for an extended period of time can be unhealthy. Even though they may come and go, we're holding onto them nonetheless, and that's not good for our mind, body, or spirit. Our irritation may be directed at someone else, a group of people or an organization, but when it comes right down to it, it ends with us.

This can show up in a number of different ways. Maybe it's about what we feel we allowed to transpire, or maybe we're upset because we stayed in a painful place longer than we feel we should have. My client Brandi said, *I put too much value in my job title and the money I was making. I allowed fear to make me think I was stuck and didn't have options. I allowed myself to live in a place that was chronically stressful, a place that was emotionally and physically draining every day. I realized working in that type of environment took time and energy from the people that meant the most to me.*

It can also be that we're in a place where we feel like we're starting over, and even though that can feel exciting, it can also feel daunting at times. Many of my clients find themselves in The Void at middle age, somewhere between 45 and 60. This can be a tough pill to swallow, at first. They often think it's too late to make a change or do something else, but what they discover is it's not too late. It's actually perfect timing, and fear has been taking over far too long. They discover it's more about allowing their heart to lead, rather than letting fear do the talking.

Forgiveness is about mercy and grace. It's a gift we give to ourselves, but I have to be honest, it's got to be one of the hardest parts of The Void that I went through during the year. Even so, I wouldn't trade it for anything, so please stick with me on this step, even if you have yet to fully step into The Void and close the door behind you. We all come out the other side at some point if we commit completely to practice the process.

I don't know how long it will take, but I do know the journey is worth the discomfort and that it means everything to how we arrive at the door out of The Void. Are we arriving as the person who came through the experience of letting go in The Void or as the person who is still struggling with letting go in The Void? Because we can find the way out by putting the steps into action, just by the sheer fact that we've committed to finding the way out, we will. That's the best news ever, right? But here's the thing, if we don't deal with the tough stuff that comes up in The Void, we take it with us. It's not that it all magically disappears once we walk out, it doesn't. It's possible to slip around in our new surroundings as we gain our footing. The difference is we'll understand how to apply the tools we've learned to make sure we don't let it sabotage our progress, because it will try.

When we're required to forgive, it means we've experienced some hurt along the way. With that hurt there's usually a loss of sorts, like giving up something we loved or a place that used to make us happy. In truth, we're talking about grief. This leads us back to the Kübler-Ross model of the Five Stages of Grief and back to Step One of Acceptance in The Void. Without acceptance, it can be difficult to let go. and that's where forgiveness comes in.

In this step, we return to our Akashic Records reading and dive into the Life Lessons, which can help us begin to connect the dots of our current path.

Life is made up of a series of experiences. Sometimes they make sense; sometimes they seem completely random. Each lifetime is about learning and soul growth while we're here on the planet. We can go through challenging experiences which are typically in line with one or two of our Life Lessons. We have a Primary Life Lesson and then some Secondary ones that we're working on in any given lifetime, and we work on them by going through experiences we planned before we arrived here. Sometimes we fight against our experiences, and therefore our lessons, because it's just too painful, and we feel lost. Other times it may seem like life is throwing us curve balls left and right, and we're holding a golf club instead of a bat, while standing three football fields away from the pitcher. It's hard to see it clearly when we're in it. It takes a heap of trust to stand in the pain while trying to find a way to take one step forward, but knowing your life lessons can be extremely beneficial and validating, which is why it's helpful to spend time connecting the dots.

When I arrived fully in The Void, I was so relieved to leave behind the stress and hurt of where I was, but there was this tape playing in the background – pretty much all the time. It was mostly comprised of replay and rehash. I'd wake up in the middle of the night and think about everything for hours. I'd review it endlessly in my mind as if somehow the amount of effort I spent thinking about it would change the outcome. I didn't even want the outcome changed. I was grateful to be free from where I was, but in reality I wasn't free at all. I was still there, trapped in my mind and the emotion du jour. My mind hadn't caught up with my heart and soul, which clearly knew where we were headed and was even excited about it. No matter how hard I tried, no matter how many Loving Kindness meditations I practiced, my mind kept returning to the past.

No matter how we arrive, whether we choose The Void reluctantly or not, it can take time to assimilate the change in our life and adjust to where we are after years of where we were. Just like in Step 1 – Acceptance, we need to be gentle with ourselves during this step and try to connect with what we need at this time, without judgment.

The emotions in this step can take some time to integrate and move through. There were moments where I'd flash back to my experience, and I was actually mad at myself for sticking around through so much pain. Then I would remind myself again that I was exactly where I was supposed to be, I'd go over all the reasons I chose to walk away, and I'd journal and pull myself into the present and where I was headed. I couldn't change the past, but I could have an incredible effect on the future. I even picked up my list of 25 Gifts I created in Tulum and wrote out how I would utilize each gift going forward. This helped remind me that it wasn't all for nothing; there were gifts along the way that I could put to use going forward.

I incorporated body work though chiropractic, massage, and yoga/stretching. The pain in my tail bone/coccyx area was a constant reminder that I needed to pay attention to my body, so I continued working on releasing that as well. At one point when the pain wasn't going anywhere, my chiropractor looked it up. Louise Hay identified coccyx (tailbone) pain emotionally as: out of balance with yourself. Holding on. Blame of self. Sitting on old pain. *You didn't have to hit me over the head or anything.* That message was loud and clear. Still, the pain hung on even though I identified and connected with it and worked to let it go every day. I knew I had to do the work and go through the process to come out the other side; to find the door to my future life. It's waiting for all of us, but we have to deal with the emotional congestion first, so we don't take it with us.

Roughly nine months after I arrived in The Void, I was still 'practicing' Loving Kindness for myself and others – *May you be happy; may you be safe; may you be healthy; may you be at peace* – but I was still struggling with twinges of anger and sadness that included thoughts about the past. It was recommended that I write a letter that I would never mail. I should say everything I always wanted to say, holding nothing back, and then burn it. I wrote the letter, and it was cathartic. I thought I would burn it immediately, but I didn't. I held onto it for four months. In the meantime, my mind continued to rehash and replay my experience again and again.

After 11 months, I found myself in the shower with the same crappy thoughts rolling around, occupying space in my mind. *You've got to be kidding me, again?* I was frustrated, but mostly I was broken. I was crushed and disgusted with myself. I couldn't spend any more time examining it. The tears began to fall. I didn't have any new insights on the same story after 11 months of picking it apart from every angle. In my defeat, I fell to my knees. Deeply crying, words spilling out of my mouth in short breaths, filling the gaps with desperation. My soul was calling out from a place I didn't recognize. I was begging for help with letting it go: *Please, I can't take it anymore. I'm exhausted and there's nothing more I can do. I've done the work. What am I missing?*

Immediately, I felt a shift, a distinct feeling of the weight being lifted. It was the moment of clarity I had been searching for all that time. In one moment I felt powerless over my mind and its ability to keep me trapped in a prison cell with my experience while it played the same scenes over and over like the movie, *Groundhog Day*. In the next, I found solace. It was in the surrender that I was released from the idea that I should've handled things differently, *read that as better,* that I had missed clues. I thought I had done something horribly wrong to cause the pain. I had created a web of confusion to be trapped in. It was odd since I had a clear desire to move on, *and* I was happy, genuinely excited about where I was headed, except my mind was interrupting me at random times to remind me I was still working on letting go. What gives?

At that moment in the shower, it finally came to me that I was most critical of myself and my part in all of it; what I had *allowed* to happen *to* me. I hadn't included *me* in the story of my forgiveness, forgetting more often than not that I truly believed it happened *for* me. The final experience that pushed me into The Void wasn't the only one the Universe sent me along the way as a sign that I wasn't where I was meant to be. My heart and soul knew it, but I wasn't listening, I was attached to the idea that I could fix it, and make it work; that it was a temporary bump and once we got past that one, we'd be back on track. Except that time never really arrived and the experiences became more intense. My Soul Calling was a massive roar when it all came tumbling down. It was so obvious that I couldn't ignore it any longer, but I stayed through one painful experience after the other. The final one was the last excruciating straw, so I would get the message, loud and clear, which I did. Then I held onto it for months after I walked away, because it was so hurtful, and I blamed myself for the pain.

Throughout those months I would intellectually recall what Louise Hay identified with coccyx pain, although it didn't integrate until that moment in the shower. I didn't understand what the pain in my butt was until I realized it was *me*. I forgot to forgive myself. I was the pain! That's when it shifted, and I began to heal on a different level. It really was incredible how the pain was lifted and the fog cleared. I was working so hard to find forgiveness for those that hurt me, I didn't realize I also needed to forgive myself for allowing myself to stay somewhere so painful for so long, for not recognizing all the signs sooner. I had some intense tapes running in my head about the experience, and it all led to my self-worth, which led me right back to my Life Lessons from my Akashic Records.

My Primary Life Lesson is Kindness. This isn't necessarily just about being kind to myself or others, what it means is I will have experiences in my life where I have the opportunity to learn about kindness from every angle. I may witness kindness through others or experience kindness from others, and I may experience its opposite. I may also learn about kindness toward the self. Our life lessons can play out in a number of different ways, but the experience that brought me into The Void gave me an up close and personal look at kindness from all sides. I tried to be gentle with myself and not beat myself up. I was hurting, and it was ok to be where I was. It was meant to be an episode, not a docudrama mini-series. In the forgiveness, I experienced the deepest kindness for myself yet.

My Secondary Life Lessons include: Forgiveness, Self-Love (*are you seeing a pattern here?*), Lightheartedness, Balance, and Sensitivity. It's almost comical to look at each one through the lens of my experience. It's validating and helps begin the process of surrender and letting go.

When we look at our Life Lessons, we often find we had the opportunity to experience one or two of them in a particularly profound event or experience. Lucky me, I had them all. Each one was present in some way throughout my situation. Make no mistake, it was excruciatingly painful at times, but honestly, the most painful parts were forcing myself to stay somewhere I was no longer meant to be. We don't have to stay stuck anywhere and truthfully, the pain continues to amp up as we allow ourselves to keep denying our soul the opportunity to be free to do what we came here to do. It's ok to let go.

And remember that letter I held onto, the one I was supposed to burn? I finally burned it on December, 21, 2016, Winter Solstice, the longest night of the year and a perfect night for letting things go.

What we learn in this step is the importance of being gentle with ourselves. It really is about letting go and continuing to move forward. Oh! And taking care of ourselves. There's that too. Which leads us to the next step.

Chapter 9

STEP 6: FOLLOW YOUR BLISS

"You know you're doing well when you lose interest in looking back."

UNKNOWN

You're going to Tulum? Oh my God, that makes me so happy. It's perfect timing. My friend and mentor, Peggy, was with me through every step leading up to and including the experience that brought me into The Void. No one understood me, or the personal energetic weight of it all, better. She knew I wore it like an old wool scarf that looked nice on the surface, but was itchy as hell. *You have to get an egg cleansing while you're there,* she said. I had no idea what that was, but I was in *yes* mode, willing to face the unknown with conviction, so I agreed.

After hours working to figure out where to have one done, I came up empty-handed. By the time we left on the trip, all I had was a restaurant called Charlie's where the owner could lead one to a healer named Maria de Tulum. I spent hours searching for a way to find Maria. I felt like I already knew her.

An egg cleansing is an ancient Shamanic healing art done by Curanderas (healers). It involves energetically clearing someone's aura so they can heal stuck energy, illness, or stress. I knew it was right for me to pursue, because I had goosebumps and felt excited the moment I heard about it. Both are indicators, for me, of being on the right track, so I took action; just like when we're Flipping Stones in Step 4. There were a number of obstacles prior to arriving, but I trusted my goosebumps. I knew it would somehow work out, that it was meant to be.

On my first full day in Tulum, I gathered my traveling companions and went to Charlie's to find Maria. The restaurant was eclectic, with interesting masks and art on one of two walls. With a wide-open front onto the sidewalk, it was great for people watching.

We hadn't been there long when a stunning woman with long black hair and a scarf over her head came gliding in. She was approaching tables and chatting with the patrons in an open, welcoming way. I felt like I was supposed to talk to her, so I followed her to the back of the restaurant. Looking back now, it makes me laugh, because I was pretty much stalking her. *Excuse me, is your name Maria?* I thought she looked a lot like the picture I'd seen online of Maria, so I broke the ice with that. It wasn't. Her name was Tanya, and we started talking about what she was doing there. *I'm looking for my friend, Charlie,* she said. I thought, *We're both looking for Charlie? This has to be a sign.* We continued chatting; at one point in our conversation, I got up the courage to say, *Do you know Maria who does egg cleansing?* I felt so insane asking her the question, but I knew I had to take action in order to find Maria. She looked confused, and then it registered, and she said, *Ah, Maria huevos – for the egg limpia, si,* she nodded and smiled. I was thrilled she knew who I was talking about. I felt like I was going to burst inside with excitement, but as she described where Maria worked, I had no idea what she was talking about. *I found a small connection to Maria, but it wasn't enough.* At least I knew she was real and not just a figment of my internet imagination. I said, *Thank you so much, Tanya.* And we exchanged a big hug.

As Tanya walked outside, she stopped to talk to a man, they were smiling and pointing at me, I knew it must be Charlie. They walked back into the restaurant together and she said, *He's going to give you Maria's number. You can't just show up at her work.* Now I was ready to break open, I was so excited.

I immediately called Maria. I was shocked when she said, *Oh, I'm not doing any egg cleansing now, I'm taking time off.* I was confused since everything happened so perfectly for me to be led to her, but she said, *I'll give you the number to Karla, she's excellent.* I regrouped and called Karla. The number didn't work at first, when I finally got through there was a language barrier and a poor connection. I knew I needed help if I was going to make it a reality.

We were staying in an Airbnb in a small neighborhood in Tulum. The owner of the rental was so helpful when we needed information, so I called him. *Hi Peppe, this is Kelli, I need help. Have you ever heard of egg cleansing?* Feeling somewhat foolish to be asking that question, I was shocked when he said he'd had one five years earlier. What are the odds? Apparently, pretty freaking good. *I'd be happy to help you,* he said, and with that he took over. He called Karla and found out she was booked, but she agreed to call him if someone cancelled.

At first I started to get down on myself for not doing more before I arrived. My confidence wavered, but there was something inside me that knew it was going to happen. I had done everything right, so I trusted that it would all work out.

I gave myself a pep talk and replayed everything up to that point. The synchronicity – Peggy, the restaurant, Tanya, Charlie, Maria, Karla, and Peppe. It was all leading somewhere, I just had to trust in my gut that it would all work out. I didn't sit around waiting for a cancellation call, I connected with the part of me that knew it was already written, and I let it go.

That next day we rode bikes to the Tulum Ruins, we sat on the beach with iguanas, we drank Thai Basil Margaritas at Mezzanine on a deck overlooking the beach, and we rode back to our home away from home. I couldn't have imagined a more perfect day. I had just finished showering when the phone rang, *There's a cancellation. I'm sending my girlfriend over in a cab, now. She's picking you up and dropping you off at Karla's gate, Karla's isn't easy to find. If you can be there in the 10 minutes, you're in.* Instantly I was nervous, excited, and a little hesitant, but I didn't have time to question what I was about to do or where I was going. There was no time to let fear take over.

The cab arrived outside and within minutes I was dropped off at an ornate gate where Karla was waiting for me. She had a welcoming energy, and she was excited that it worked out, *It was meant to be, yes?* I smiled. *Absolutely*, I said, still feeling the fluttering in my stomach. We walked across the yard dotted with roosters and chickens as she led me into the one-room hut for the cleansing.

It was a beautiful ceremony with prayer, smudging, and two, uncooked eggs in the shell. I stood on a mat while she placed the first egg in the smoke and then rubbed it over my clothed body. She continually spoke a prayer in Spanish, which I didn't understand. Later, she said, *I asked for clarity and healing for you.* The second egg was in my right hand. When she was done, she tapped the first egg on the four corners of a glass, cracked it open and dropped the yolk into the water. She told me what she saw in the egg. She said, *I don't see you at first, but then you appeared,* she laughed, *like you popped onto the scene, because you were hiding.* She points to the bubbles in the water, *All those bubbles, they represent too much in the mind, too much thought.* I laughed.

She went to the second egg and that's where it got even more interesting. She described the painful experience I'd had before I walked away completely into The Void, even down to the people involved. It was amazing. *We will leave this here in the glass,* she said, as we both laughed with the knowledge that I didn't have to take them with me. After she was done, I felt noticeably lighter, like I was free from the weight of the experience. I had clarity. I even felt safe, which was so interesting to me, because I was dropped off by a stranger at a gate where I had never been in the middle of Tulum. I didn't know how I was going to return to my rental, and it was now dark outside. I knew we hadn't driven far, but for me, the feeling of being alone in a strange country, where I didn't speak the language and I had no idea how I was going to get back, usually wouldn't elicit feelings of safety or clarity. But something shifted, and I found my courage in Tulum. And it started with the egg cleansing. I can only describe it as being willing to let go and do things differently in the name of reconnecting with my soul and spirit.

I knew I was supposed to be at the egg cleansing, I was certain it would happen. I knew I was seeking healing for myself that was 100% in alignment with my soul. There was incredible synchronicity to make it all possible for me to find Karla, and I wasn't going to allow anything to take away the rekindled awareness that I had the power to co-create and make things happen, if I trusted and let go of how they happen.

I've always known this, and I've manifested so many incredible things in my life. But there were times when I was also waiting for the other shoe to drop. Incredible things happened all the time, and then I'd wait around for it to all implode, scared to enjoy them fully. I'd let fear tell me it wasn't wise to completely feel the joy. There wasn't a lot of possibility for enjoying the ride or fully experiencing the adventure in the moment. I was ten steps ahead of myself, worried about something that may never happen and was totally out of my control or completely fabricated by my mind. It was no way to live. In the adventure of the egg cleansing, I healed more than my energetic body. I healed the connection to my soul.

I'm telling you about this now, because I want to make a point in how we approach this step, because in this step we create what I call a Soul Care Plan. We create it by identifying what our soul may be needing to feel nurtured, healed, or cared for, and then we commit to it and enjoy everything it offers in the moment, even if we go on an adventure to find it. We may not even know what it is we're seeking. We may just have a notion about what we want to accomplish, like healing or clearing out stuck energy.

Part of my Soul Care Plan involved going to Tulum to reconnect with myself again and to start the process of healing from the experience that brought me into The Void. At first I didn't know what that meant, but once I identified it as being an egg cleansing, I went on that adventure, even though I was hesitant at first. I followed the path as it unfolded in front of me. I knew energy work would help, because it had in the past. Your Soul Care Plan will align with your soul, but don't be afraid to try something new, like an egg cleansing, if it feels right.

Originally, I called this step *Take Care of Yourself,* but it really wasn't enough, because this step is about going deeper. This step involves amping up from self-care to soul care. Soul care is about nurturing our whole self: mind, heart, and soul. It asks that we be willing to step out of our comfort zone to find what will help us continue on our journey of soul connection and spiritual healing. There's a little bit of magic, self-discovery, and motivation in this step.

Once we understand what we're trying to do here, it can be motivating to figure out what might make our soul soar. It can be an entirely new way to look at the unknown with excitement for what's ahead rather than confusion or even nausea. Please don't be deterred by this step. There will be a number of firsts along this journey, and soul care is just another form of exploration. I promise this step can be fun, no worries here.

Let's talk about the importance of this step.

No matter what experience brings us into The Void, there's a good possibility it was demanding of our time, energy, and emotions. Maybe it took everything we had to show up as the person we know ourselves to be. Once we walk away, we realize we didn't stop to ask what *we* needed, because we were busy focusing on everything else.

Once we're in The Void, we can look for new stressors and struggles to work through, because that's what we're used to feeling. That's exactly what we're trying to avoid in this step, so we connect to our soul. It's about taking care of ourselves on the level of our soul, like with an egg cleansing. This is not unlike setting intentions and making commitments. In fact, we often set some soul care intentions and commitments for ourselves in Step 3 – *Direct your Drive,* without even realizing it.

It may not be easy at first to figure out what makes us feel good when we're looking to take care of ourselves on the soul level. It might be hard to express how we like to be taken care of, especially what we might allow ourselves to receive in the name of feeling deeply good. Add in the element that we're caring for our soul as well as the heart and mind, and it can become difficult to identify at first, but once we get going, it's possible to enjoy the process of listening to our soul's desires. The idea is to write it down and then explore it for resonance, just like we did in Step 4, Flipping Stones. We create the Soul Care Plan, and then we commit to go on the adventure of where that plan may take us. This is the fun part. It's all about trust, synchronicity, co-creating, play, and feeling in alignment. The outcome can include healing, release, centeredness, strength, and fierce connection. In this step, we're encouraged to take some time to really dive into what we feel would be nourishing for our soul. Is it massage, some type of body or energy work, a regular yoga practice, tai-chi, craniosacral therapy, or soul nurturing vacations – if so, how often and where? Since some of the activities aren't easily accessible, like traveling on a soul nurturing trip, we also create what's called a Soul Care List. This list includes some indulgence and juicy love for ourselves; it includes the easier *go-to* activities we can turn to when we're feeling disconnected, sad, lonely, or stuck in our heads.

My client Athena's Soul Care List included things like, *drink tea, listen to Indian flute music, go to an artist workshop, float in the ocean, play in the alpine flowers, connect with my community, visit my grandma, tend my garden.* She created a gorgeous draft of incredibly soul-sensual things she could access to connect deeply with the nurturing desires from her soul, when she allows for it.

This is the list we use to create the Soul Care Plan, but we don't discard the activities that don't transfer to the bigger plan. It becomes the rescue list, the things we can turn to in times of need or to reconnect with ourselves. Things that don't have to be scheduled, that are more easily accessible than getting on a plane to Tulum to find yourself again. Typically that takes some planning, so we need some activities we can initiate to get right with ourselves because there are times when we will get off track.

The Soul Care Plan could include getting out of the country for rest, relaxation, and spiritual exploration. This could mean new bodywork experiences or visiting high vibrational destinations, spiritual powerhouse areas where we may be drawn to recharge the soul. It might even include a retreat or life-changing experience with a well-known coach, like Tony Robbins's *Date with Destiny*. It's ok if we're not really sure when or how, we just put it on there.

The Soul Care Plan can be a little less specific, which is why we create the Soul Care List first. The list is the specifics, and the plan has a broader focus of what we'd like to accomplish when it comes to soul care, since we may not know the *how*, yet. We'll be guided, but we have to identify the *what* first, just like we did when we were setting intentions and making commitments in Step 3, Direct Your Drive.

In my Soul Care Plan for 2016, I simply said, *Reconnect with my soul, release hurt,* and *heal my body.* I wasn't even specific about how that would happen. I put it down and remained open to where that would take me, and I followed the roadmap to the egg cleansing in Tulum.

When we're in pain, stuck in our heads, or beating ourselves up, we can latch onto something tangible to get us out of our funk. We can choose anything from our Soul Care List to easily get back in alignment. Athena can *drink tea, listen to Indian flute music, or play in the Alpine flowers.* She can make any of those things happen without a ton of effort. I can jump in my car, open up the sunroof, blast Prince on the stereo, head up the coast, and catch a sunset. That's on my Soul Care List, and it works. This is in lieu of saying, *I'm just going to sit and stew in my crap.*

The cool caveat is, sometimes we don't actually have to do it. There are times where just the idea of it, like Athena's *touch the ocean* or my *walking in the giant Redwoods,* can bring about a shift. Sometimes we can just recall what it feels like to do the activity, thinking, *What's on my list? What are the things I can do that are the juicy indulgences for my soul?* Depending on the situation, we can feel a shift just by aligning our thoughts with the activities we've identified as soul nurturing.

In this step, we think about our Soul Care Plan and where we'd like to go; who we'd like to see; what we want to create. How are we going to take care of ourselves on the soul level? It's powerful to approach self-care in this deeper way. Are you ready?

Chapter 10
STEP 7: MIND THE MIND

"Make sure your worst enemy doesn't live between your own two ears."

LAIRD HAMILTON, *American big wave surfer*

At 26, I was young and waking up after walking into AA. I worked for years to stuff my pain deep inside me where I thought I wouldn't have to deal with it. I hid it behind a fortress, behind the surface emotions of sarcasm and a forced smile. I was angry, deeply furious really, about my life and where I was. I didn't think twice about how I talked to myself. Sometimes I was encouraging, mostly I was degrading.

I felt lost after suffering through the outcomes of the adult choices I'd made in my teens. I was judgmental and constantly fighting with where I wanted to be. Where I wanted to be was happy, not in my mind happy, but happy in my heart and spirit. I never thought I would find it.

I sought happiness outside of myself; hence the men, drinking, and drugs. I was constantly filled with anxiety. I thought, if I could just escape the judgment of my mind and ignore the heart-breaking pain in my soul, if I just kept moving forward in spite of myself, then I might not die that day.

This step is about noticing our thoughts and choosing to manage them, even change them, when they aren't serving us. It's about learning how to get the hell out of our heads for our own good. This requires a little bit of diligence and being open to expanding the mind. When we trust in our heart and soul direction, we can engage our mind to creatively lead us to where we're meant to be, but our thoughts need to be useful rather than a barrier.

Let's start with the less than helpful thoughts that may be coursing through our mind throughout the day. When we first start noticing the rhetoric going on in there, it's all we can do to tell ourselves to *let it go*. Whether we listen or not is another thing. We can be our own worst critic, our biggest impediment to growth, and a huge obstacle when we want to try something new. Much of this can happen without consciously realizing it. What if our mind was on board, cheering us on instead of getting in the way and breaking us down? But how do we make that happen?

We can work on this by becoming aware of our thoughts and what they're telling us, especially where it relates to our fears.

Once we realize everything we want is on the other side of The Void, but we're required to go through our fear to get to it, we become aware of how much our fear has been stopping us from following our heart and creating the life of our dreams. We approach this step by becoming aware of the impact the mind has on our life when it's running amuck.

We can have approximately 60,000 different thoughts a day. That leaves a lot of opportunity for them to be less than helpful, to actually impede our journey and throw detours in our way. This can be especially tricky, because our physical body reacts to our thinking, which is why it's so important to be able to check in on what we're feeling and see if it's a product of what we're thinking, especially when it's negative.

The mind is a crafty bugger. If we aren't in control of our mind, then the mind can easily be in control of us. Getting a handle on our thoughts, especially the ones that are driven by the internal judge and jury, can be a 24/7 operation in the beginning. It gets easier with practice, diligence, and the willingness to be free from the power of being taken on a pessimistic *joy* ride by our mind, especially since there's nothing joyous about it.

When we learn to spot it and pivot before it has time to mutate, we're on our way to changing the behavior, but we have to become aware before we can shift.

Of those 60,000 thoughts we think in a day, it's said 90% of those are on repeat AND of those repeating thoughts, 80% are geared toward the negative. That's right, it's not our fault that, at times, our worst enemy is in fact living between our own two ears. It's not a cruel mind trick the Universe has played on us. It actually served us pretty well centuries ago when we were on high alert watching out for anything that wanted to eat us, like a saber-toothed tiger. So we're predisposed to this type of thinking, but one of the best ways out of the cycle, I've found, is to question it.

Even though I understand how this works, it still took me a long time to become proficient at breaking the cycle of negative thoughts. It still trips me up at times, but I'm much faster to pivot these days.

If we want to shift our reality, then we need to understand that not everything we're thinking is meant to be accepted without question. It's almost like our mind is a grade school bully who spreads vicious rumors in order to validate its existence. Typically, we just want to get away from the bully, but we really need to stand up to it, get in there, and question the message. So in this step we become conscious of what our mind has to say – what's negatively playing on replay and rehash, and we question the relevance.

When we first start to do this, it's like a giant spotlight turns the focus on the dark crevices in our mind, the parts we never really wanted to visit, but we have to identify what's happening in there in order to deal with it. It's uncomfortable to shine the light on the unhealthy thoughts passing through. I visualize this like the Stock Exchange ticker tape. The streaming stock symbols and numbers endlessly traveling across the screen. It's fast and overwhelming trying to keep up, and at some point, it starts over again. Unfortunately, when we want to get out of our heads, we can find ourselves in there at an increased rate, but we may not be doing any good other than listening to the streaming negativity. The problem comes in when we believe it.

Our mind can be a terrible neighborhood to get lost in. My mind can be creative, harsh, and beautiful all at the same time. It comes up with some crazy stuff. I've spent countless hours questioning its motives and checking in on its accuracy. When we question what it's telling us, we begin to become aware of the storyline it's running. But without diligence and practice, it's hard to stop that Stock Exchange ticker tape. It just keeps rolling along with symbols and numbers.

When we're feeling negative or doubtful, there might be some automatic thoughts on the ticker tape that need to be challenged. The bully may be running its mouth and spreading nasty rumors. When we question our thoughts, we begin to see them for what they are, just a thought, and we have the opportunity to choose a different one. It takes vigilance and patience. It's not something that happens overnight, but it's worth any amount of effort we're willing to put in.

We can't talk about minding the mind without discussing worry. I think I've cornered the market on worry in my life. I touched on this in Chapter 2 – *Survey the Landscape*, and this is where we're going deeper.

My mind was a superstar when it came to worrying. I've actually worried about how much I worry. Worrying takes a lot of energy. For a year I had a sign in my office that said, *Worrying never changes the outcome.* I knew I spent time worrying about things completely out of my control, like what other people thought about me, whether employees were happy, if I was making a difference. These were thoughts I traced from a negative feeling in my body back to my mind, then was required to examine them and pivot out of the emotions or stay stuck in the discomfort. I had a choice to buy into what they were saying or talk myself through it, because in reality what was underlying my self-defeating thoughts at that time was fear. Fear of failure, and, as I discovered, it was also fear of success. It wasn't every moment of every day, but it was on the ticker tape, passing through. I would hear it and feel it, but I wasn't necessarily doing anything about it, so it became repetitive and grew stronger.

Even when things are great we can spend a lot of time swirling in worry. I learned to get out of my head by questioning the message and pulling myself through. This took time and energy. It took applying myself and dedicating time to unravel the Christmas lights. There wasn't any truth to what I was hearing, but I needed to spot it and eradicate it, sometimes repetitively, because it would come back around again, just like the ticker tape.

One of the best tools I've found to Mind the Mind is having a solid spiritual practice. Why is this so important? Because we can do the work, but still be stuck in the negative distortion, which translates to churning in a painful existence where so much of the focus can be toward what we *think* is going on rather than what is *actually* going on. We can focus on what we believe *might* be happening, instead of all the amazing stuff that *is* happening. There are typically amazing parts in our experiences, even the painful ones, we just have to be able to recognize them even when we're caught up in our negative thinking. Our heart can see the gentler side. It can see the value in our life experiences. But if we aren't adept at dropping into our heart when our mind is going off, it can be tormenting.

When things are going well, it's easy to want to kick our feet up and relax, but when it all hits the fan and we run into a challenge, that's when we find out what we're made of. Having survival tools in place can be key. The idea is to create a foundation for ourselves to rely on when the tough stuff comes up, because it will continue to arise once we walk out of The Void.

Throughout the steps, we're adding different tools into our toolbox. Each of them helps with this step in some way. Having acceptance about where we are in the practice to get hold of our thoughts, is important. Forgiving ourselves for listening and believing the negative dialogue in our mind is also right up there too. We can also tap into the FEAR Method in this step. That tool alone can quickly get us into the process of modifying our thoughts and beliefs about a certain situation. When we feel fear arise, we imagine the little child pulling on our coat, and in that moment, we stop to Face, Embrace, Accept, Release, and Shift. Many of our negative beliefs are certainly based in fear, but we're building quite a little arsenal in the toolbox to blow our mind-bully to bits. There are some additional tools and concepts we can use for lasting transformation.

It's important to become our own champion. I mentioned earlier that we have another voice besides the bully, one that's on our side, that's willing to stand up and say how things *truly* are. It can see clearly all the good aspects of who we are. This is our internal champion or coach. We can tap into this when we find ourselves banging our heads with bats or running a negative narrative. We can connect to our heart and put the bully in its place with some positive self-talk. We don't have to believe everything our mind is telling us. It's not easy at first; it takes practice. It can even feel a little cheesy when we first start to be our own coach, but with time, we can come to appreciate that voice inside who has our back and wants us to succeed. The voice that says, *Hey, this might be a possibility* instead of, *What the hell are you thinking?* There's true power in positivity.

The next tool is meditation. Hold on, don't skip to the next chapter. I get it. Meditation is everywhere, it must be totally overrated, right? Here's the thing, I'm not going to say we *must* meditate in The Void, but I will say why it's worth it to get past the story we have about how difficult or sucky it is. That said, it's up to each of us to feel our way through meditation and our own connection to a personal practice.

If someone says we have to meditate and we sit on a cushion for however long we deem necessary and the mind has its way with us, then we're not really getting the full benefit anyway. Sure, there's value in taking time for ourselves, but the real value comes when we practice mindfulness by gently bringing the focus back to our practice when the mind has wandered.

We meditate in The Void so we can build a relationship with ourselves, so we become more aware and understand how easy it is to get off track, because the mind wants to take us on that joyless joyride. Even though we may understand all the physical benefits like reduced stress or anxiety, no one can make us meditate. In my experience, we get it when we get it.

Meditation can be something we resist. The body and mind aren't accustomed to meditating, so it feels uncomfortable in the beginning. When we decide to do something differently we don't want to feel that annoying feeling. Our mind believes it knows better, and we get a running dialogue from our inner critic about how hard it is, because it doesn't want us to break away and create something new. It wants us to stay comfortable, *read that as stuck*, because it's cozy and safe there, and that's what it knows.

Meditating puts the focus on us. Typically in the beginning it's putting the focus directly on our thoughts. When we're alone with those thoughts, they can be unruly, useless, and even frustrating. Unhinging ourselves from the thought monkey is difficult at first. We have to be ok with feeling the discomfort of meditating, because we have this idea that we should be totally Zen while were doing it. Cue the eye roll. I completely understand, I promise.

I went through yoga teacher training 20 years ago. In it we took a deep dive into the practice and its history; we also meditated. We journaled about our daily practice, which included daily asanas (poses) and meditation. I was re-sis-tant! I fought it. I look back on those journals, and I can see that I was uncomfortable. It never really settled in for me. I did it, and even felt better after I did it, but I didn't like it. I was like a little kid, kicking and screaming. After I became certified to teach, I stopped my daily meditation practice, even though intellectually I understood all the benefits. I created a practice for myself that I called a *walking meditation*. I linked my breath to my everyday travels of walking from one place to the next. I made the connection of the breath to reduction of stress and my overall health, but I didn't want to sit and *be* for an extended period of time, because I couldn't quiet my mind and it was painful to know I had no control over it, which put the focus on the thought that *my mind was just one more thing I had no control over*. Add it to the list. Sneaky, right? This is exactly why we practice meditation, but my mind convinced me that I didn't have enough patience to do it. So I created a work-around, my walking meditation practice.

It worked for a long time. I became stronger at managing those trigger moments, but my mind got stronger in how it talked to me, it became more vigilant as I became more centered. I was still stuck in my head more often than not. If we want to have a fighting chance with this step, we need to understand what works and then put it into action, just like when we're Flipping Stones in Step 4. I like to look at meditation as just another stone to turn in the name of winning the battle with the bully in our heads. If we want more command over our thoughts and reactions, if we want to be less fearful and speak up compassionately when something really matters, while not caring what someone thinks of us, meditation can help with all of this.

Meditation helped me gain clarity, find my joy, manage my emotions, keep fear at bay, and open myself back up fully to my intuition. In Chapter 9, I talked about the idea of waiting for the other shoe to drop, where my mind was saying, *Yes, things seem well and good right now, but just wait. It will eventually come crashing down, and you'll be sorry you spent time excited about it. So you might as well be prepared and not fully enjoy it. Let's stay right here and avoid the pain of what's to come, avoid the disappointment.*

When we believe the other shoe is going to drop, we're believing in the reality that we can't be fully joyous about an experience, our life, or where we're headed. It's about fear, because yes, it's possible to have a fear of being too happy, so we stay in what we know. If we don't get too excited, we don't have to face the extreme disappointment when it all comes crashing down. We pre-plan our pain threshold before we even know where that excitement wanted to take us.

Fear can be so destructive in its desire to protect us from perceived trouble. This is why we spend time in The Void learning to Mind the Mind. The idea that we can't fully enjoy our successes, experiences, or relationships, because at some point they're going to implode anyway, is discouraging and self-defeating, but so many of us think just like that. Our brains are wired this way. It's not our fault, but we want to understand, if we don't identify as the person who's in control of managing our mind in the tough times, it will continue to manage us.

My client, Brandi was acutely aware of her inner dialogue when we first started working together. She said, *It wants me to believe that I won't be successful and that I don't know what I'm doing. It wants me to believe I'm not worthy of living the life of my dreams.* It doesn't take much for us to be aware of the way our thoughts work to stop us from making fulfilling choices in our lives, choices in alignment with our heart and soul.

Brandi checked in after practicing daily meditation for a few weeks and realized that it was an important piece that was missing from her life. She felt more grounded and centered in all areas of her life. She was hopeful and excited for the future after months of doubting her direction and feeling defeated. This is part of the *solid spiritual practice* I mentioned at the beginning of the chapter.

When we first begin a meditation practice, we're in a place where we're open to getting to know ourselves as a soul. We're working on the most sacred relationship of all, the one with ourselves. This is somewhere our mind has no business butting in and getting involved, yet it can be the most challenging part of meditating, which is why it's a practice.

It might be helpful to spend a little time exploring different meditation techniques and see what resonates, It's not a one size fits all for sure. I also recommend checking out YouTube or the Calm App for some guided meditations. I use the Calm App every day and it's made a huge difference in my personal practice.

When we Mind the Mind, we're open to Flipping Stones just like we did in Chapter 4. We practice the tools and see what works, but we don't give up because it feels hard or we're frustrated. We remain open to the idea that we can meditate, that the mind bully will be tamed or our internal coach can be a valuable resource. Any choices we make in this step is progress toward living a more peaceful and heart-centered life.

Chapter 11
STEP 8: INVEST IN YOURSELF

"If you don't build your dream, someone will hire you to build theirs."

TONY A. GASKINS, JR., *The Dream Chaser*

Money is hard to get! That's what my client Athena said in one of our first few sessions. I knew exactly why she felt this way, but we had to work through her destructive beliefs about money in order to get her to where she wanted to be in her life, to what she had envisioned as we worked together.

The word *invest* conjures up images of banks, stocks, finance, or money. Any one of these things might bring up stressful feelings for us, because our mind has a story we tell ourselves about them, especially money. *We don't have enough money to feel at peace. We need more to feel stable. When I have $10,000 in the bank, I'll feel content. When I make enough money, I can do what I want to do or pursue my dreams.*

We feel caught in a cycle of earn it and burn it, because money seems to come and go so quickly. *But is that a bad thing, really?* The fact that it's coming is definitely good, but the fact that it's going may not be so bad either. What matters is what we're spending it on.

It's important in The Void to explore what it means to invest in ourselves. If we love what we're doing, we may be more accepting of our account balance. If we're spending money on our spiritual growth or on fulfilling our dreams, we might feel more content than we've ever felt, even with less money under our mattress.

Back in the mid-90s, I read Shakti Gawain's book, *Creative Visualization,* and it changed my life. But I still carried around an underlying fear of not having enough money to feel secure. More often than not, I'd get in my own way where money was concerned. *I'll feel better when I make more money, like six figures* – I didn't. *I'll feel better if I own a house* – I didn't. *I'll feel better if we have a 401k, investments, savings... stability.* I didn't. It didn't matter if we had money or not, I felt exactly the same way, and I told myself the same inadequate story about it. I realized I was just as afraid of not having money, as I was about losing it, when I did. Once I began to manifest what I wanted in my life, I had to turn the focus on myself and get to the heart of my fears about being destitute. Which I was never really close to being, *ever.* It wasn't always easy, but I was always taken care of, even if I was sleeping on a friend's couch or moving side rolls in a hay field in exchange for a free RV parking space. Learning that it was ok to invest in myself, without having some feeling of scarcity or guilt about it, was the biggest hurdle of all.

This is the final step along the journey of creating the Destiny Roadmap. This step is the last puzzle piece we put in place so we can begin to live the life we're meant to live.

With this step we have everything we need to navigate along our Destiny Roadmap with precision, trust, and guidance. We have the ability to recognize the sign posts and follow the map by traveling the course with ease and patience, even if the course takes a detour here and there. There's sure to be a lesson in that detour, if we're willing to look for it.

This step could be overlooked, because it might not seem as important as the others, but it is important. Throughout the entire process, we've been investing in ourselves in some way. We're not only looking at monetary examples or ideas here; investing in The Void is about *participating, empowering, providing,* and yes, sometimes *spending.*

When we *participate* we're invested in whatever we're doing. We give ourselves permission to be engaged in our life and co-create with the Universe. We participate in some way in each step. When we look back at the steps, we work on Acceptance & Forgiveness. We learn a new way of facing our fears with the FEAR Method. We set Intentions and make Commitments and take action on them by Flipping Stones. We create a Soul Care Plan and hopefully commit to Mind the Mind, by noticing what's on repeat and rehash in there. We participate in each step in some way.

When we *empower* ourselves in The Void, we're encouraged and inspired to go after what we want. We're investing in the possible, in what can happen when we let go completely into our lives and trust that we're on a path of learning and experiencing aligned with our soul. It can feel empowering to set the course and take action, now that we know how.

When we *provide* what we need in The Void, we take care of ourselves. The Soul Care Plan is all about providing for our soul and what it requires to grow and shine. We're feeding, replenishing, and offering everything we've identified along the way as being necessary for our continued growth. Once we've discovered what that is, we want to nurture it by committing to our Soul Care Plan.

In The Void, we invest in ourselves personally. It's really what the entire journey is about, working on the most important relationship in our lives, the one with ourselves. This can happen in so many different ways. It's ok to take time to reconnect or to spend money on our soul desires and wishes. We save up, if we have to, but we make it happen. We make memories now, not someday in the future. We came here to experience our lives, so let's truly live. It's not only a place for learning, it's also a place for exploring and enjoying. When the mind jumps in to derail us, we go ahead and tell it to butt out, as best we can.

After I had an egg cleansing, climbed a pyramid, and swam in a Cenote with bats in Tulum, the idea that I also needed a massage popped into my head. At first I questioned the intel, because I don't get a lot of massages. Energetically, they aren't easy for me to process. Truthfully, I was also scared to crash the elation and clarity I had from the trip so far, from everything I'd felt I'd done right to get me where I was. Layer that with spending more money on the trip, and I had huge reservations, but I checked in again and knew it wasn't to be ignored. My intuition said, *Trust and push through the hesitation.* I knew deep down I could use more help with releasing and getting back in touch with myself, so I looked online for someone who resonated with my soul – *a massage with someone who understands energy.* That was my actual internet search, and it was obvious who the right person was as soon as I opened the link to his business and read the reviews from his former clients.

I arrived at Animamente in late afternoon. I felt the nervous energy swirling inside me as I sat down with Marco to chat. Eventually he asked me why I came to see him. *I'm in Tulum to reconnect with myself again. I need someone to get the stress and stuck energy out of me, I need someone to empty it all out.* In a gentle voice, layered with an accent, he said, *if you trust me, I can do that. I have a gift, but only in what the person allows me to do.* My heart soared when his words settled on me. *I trust you,* I said through a hesitant smile. In reality, I was nervous. Fear was rising up into my throat, finding its way into my head or maybe it was the other way around, but the message was clear, *run!* I had no idea who Marco was, but deep down I could feel his loving support even just sitting next to him, but my mind persisted. I found him online, in Mexico, and it's getting dark outside. I heard my internal pessimist say, *It's too expensive anyway.* I answered back with only one thought: *I've been led here for a reason. Everything about this trip has been amazing. Trust! This will be too.*

In the two-hour massage, I was transported, cradled, and cared for in a way I have never experienced in my life. There was incredible beauty in what transpired. When it was over I felt like we traveled through time and space together and back.

After I got dressed, I felt at peace, and I was amazed that I really did feel like he emptied me out. There was something missing, in the best way possible. I thought we were done, but as I was walking out of the massage room, he turned me around and placed my face in the palm of his hands. They were soft and warm. I wasn't quite sure what was happening, but he looked deep into my eyes and said, *My dear, your energy is beautiful, in a gentle peaceful way,* heavy sigh, *but your mind is a mess.* I still laugh at his brutal honesty, he wanted so much for me to hear him in that moment. *I know,* I said. He was right, I felt it in my heart. I hadn't been consistently taking care of myself for years. I'd been working so hard in my job, often neglecting my soul connection. In that moment I made an internal commitment to focus everything I had on getting a handle on it.

When the Universe wants us to really understand something or get a message, it will find any way it can to communicate its importance. Marco was the spiritual wake-up call I needed to fully integrate the previous step of Mind the Mind. I was meditating every day while I was in Tulum, and I wanted to continue when I got back, but we know how it goes when it comes to taking care of ourselves. I had to commit fully.

Marco wasn't done: *It's important to make choices based on what is going to fill you and your soul and the money will come. You are good at making money, stop worrying about that.* In that intimate moment with my face in his hands, he said, *Kelli, choose wisely, go away from being the one who is in charge of all those people.* I humbly said, *I left my job.* He said, *Yes, that's a start,* as he gently pulled me closer to rest my forehead on his. *I have emptied you out, it's now up to you what you put back in.* Those words echoed through every cell in my body. It was always up to me what I put in, but now I was *clear*, and I needed to be consciously aware of maintaining that clarity.

It doesn't necessarily take someone like Marco to empty us out (although if you're in Tulum, don't miss the opportunity), we all need to be cognizant of what we put in, every day. What are we feeding ourselves, literally and figuratively? How do we keep shining brightly? How do we maintain our connection? Are we investing in ourselves and our soul in positive ways?

Marco's messages have stayed with me. I took his words to heart. In my journal I wrote, in part, *Clearly I'm at the beginning again.* It was in that moment that I committed to live my truth and no longer hide who I am from the world. It was time to come out of the spiritual closet and let go of my fears, especially where money was concerned. Imagine if I had listened to that voice that told me I'd already spent enough money on the trip, and it was self-indulgent to spend more on a massage. What if I'd allowed my fear to win, and I walked out of his place, never having the gift of going on that journey with him? Thankfully, I knew enough to understand why I was in Tulum, and the Universe led me to Marco. The deep healing and life-changing experiences can be rare, but they can happen more often when we strengthen the trust in our internal guidance. I would have paid ten times what he charged, but I didn't know that going in. I had to trust in where I was being led. Once again, honoring the synchronicity and the signs.

When I started examining how I felt about money throughout my life, I realized something important to begin the process of finally healing my worries where money was concerned. I was always investing in myself in some way. Even in my 20s when I was living in NYC in a tiny apartment, I was continually sending myself the message that I didn't have enough money when, in reality, I always managed to find ways to spend money in the name of my spiritual growth. I went to regular body work sessions and therapy to get my head on straight – it didn't really accomplish that, but I went for a number of years anyway. I went to a past-life regression therapist, ate organic food, and bought self-help books, I spent money on myself even when I didn't think I had it. I found a way, because I knew it was important for my growth. I could do it by myself, but I knew it would be faster, and I'd be more successful, if I had help.

Money can be a huge block for many of us. Even if we understand the principles of co-creating; whether we have money saved up or not.

Just like me, I've seen friends and clients who stress over money and their bank accounts, even when they're in great shape. At times, I still catch myself believing the story my mind wants to tell me about money. This is where the mind is so crafty, there are moments where it's still possible to find myself right back in the fear, and I pull myself into my heart and the reality of where I am, which in that moment is perfectly taken care of. I always have been. Just like my husband Joe says, *It's just money, we'll make more.* It's funny, when we first met, it annoyed me when he said that, because I didn't trust my money-making abilities. It took me a while, but eventually that thought helped me let go of my restrictive, lacking beliefs about money.

If we do what we're passionate about, the money will follow. We've all heard that statement, but I've seen plenty of people who are following their passions, and then they decide they have to give in and go back to whatever they were doing before. Does that mean they weren't passionate enough? Did they connect with the wrong passion? Wrong time, wrong location, or wrong place? Maybe, maybe not. Perhaps they had energetic hang-ups about money or they didn't invest in themselves to understand beyond just having a deep passion. Perhaps they had a fear of failure or a fear of success. Maybe they missed the signs along the way that were pointing them in the right direction. There are any number of things that can contribute to success or failure either way; sometimes people quit right before they make the breakthrough. It's so hard to know for sure.

It could be they put all their eggs in the wrong basket. Through the creation of my own Destiny Roadmap, I realized my eggs could be in a bunch of different baskets, because my happiness didn't reside in just one passion. We can make room for everything we love, even the enjoyable parts we carry with us out of the experience that brought us into The Void. The parts that make it hard to walk away, those can be included in our new future on the other side of The Void, because I've found them to typically be in line with one or two of our Soul Gifts and other aspects of our Akashic Records.

Once we make the connection, we begin to see why they feel so aligned, and we make room for those talents in our lives in some way. Often, it brings money. It just happens. I've seen it occur again and again, especially in my own life. I didn't have to completely walk away from everything I knew and loved, by remaining open to the journey it all came together in way I could have never imagined. At some point one of our passions may come to the forefront more than the others, but the idea here is we don't push anything away because we have an idea of what we think life should look like. When we understand our Soul Gifts, we have the ability to align our life in a way that feels easy and fulfilling, albeit maybe a little untraditional.

Coaching is at the heart of my soul, and it's one of my Soul Gifts. I have a second Soul Gift I utilize in my coaching practice, it's called Inspirer/Motivator. This gift is about showing others what's possible for them, to help them see the bigger picture and hold energy for them by tapping into what hasn't happened yet. I hold that space for clients, until they can see it for themselves.

Perhaps the Soul Gift I've utilized the most in my life is that of Catalyst for Change – I'm not someone who has typically shied away from change, *heights yes, change, no.* I can see this gift in the varied experiences I've had over the years. I've lived in five states and been willing to follow where spirit has led me, even when I had no idea what was ahead, no matter how much fear I had. I've been co-creating my life with the Universe for decades. Change can be good, but no matter how many times you hear that, you may not *buy in.*

What I've learned is we have to be open to change in order to accept it, and many people are deeply afraid of it. Those with the Soul Gift of Catalyst for Change are skilled in the art of change and transformation. I'm not afraid of the rat's nest or disorder, because I know it typically occurs before *big* and, often, amazing changes happen. There's usually a message in the turmoil, like a Soul Calling. That message sometimes helps push us toward the biggest growth and changes in our lives. That's the reason I feel so alive when I'm coaching or doing readings. They encompass many of my Soul Gifts. They align perfectly, and knowing this helped me envision my Destiny Roadmap in the Void.

I helped me see how I could incorporate all of my Soul Gifts in my life in a complete and undivided way. It weaved together so much of what I enjoyed and where I excelled into a seamless path, but no one could tell me how to do it like this.

My roadmap helps me make better decisions, because I understand where my soul will feel most aligned. There is additional information in a soul's Akashic Records that we utilize to create a client's Destiny Roadmap. We're only discussing a couple of them in this book, for ease of understanding. The roadmap is a living, evolving map, but what doesn't change in this lifetime is our past, our gifts. The roadmap will always be changing, because new information will be added to it as we make choices, grow and follow the guidance. As we become more skilled at co-creating, we'll be modifying what we want to create and include in our intentions and commitments.

When we're open to going on the journey and enjoying the ride, we release any preconceived ideas of what our lives are supposed to look like. We co-create based on our heart connection and not the mind, because the mind wants to get in there and tell us it can't be done in the way we're being shown. We want to *ease* into our lives by understanding we are limitless, life is limitless, and co-creating is limitless. We are only limited by what we tell ourselves.

My client Brandi is co-creating a life she loves, with enough time for her grandkids and herself. Her working life now utilizes two of her Soul Gifts: Improving & Maximizing Systems and Coaching. She feels 100% aligned with the work she's doing, and it's on her terms. She doesn't take home any of the stress she used to with her old job, and she's held onto the aspects of the job she enjoyed, like training and creating efficient systems. She's opened her own business, while she's also doing consulting work.

During the creation of her Destiny Roadmap, she identified the 25 gifts she received from her previous job, and we matched them up with information from her Akashic Records, which gave her the validation and confidence to be open to exploring opportunities that didn't look like anything she could have imagined.

My client Athena utilized her Akashic Records information and her Soul Gifts of Problem Solving, Management & Organization and Artist by creatively redesigning the business she had already been operating for eight years. She described the process as *looking at it through a window she never knew was there.* She was able to open up her vision for her business to include all the things she wanted to incorporate into her life. It unfolded in a plan that has her working on the creation of her vision and hosting events in line with her revamped company. Some of the investment in her vision required no money whatsoever, just a new perspective and trust in herself. She's crafting a new vision for a company that aligns with her heart and soul, and she's excited about what she's already accomplished and how she feels about her life.

In the beginning she thought she had to end her working partnership with her sister because she found it increasingly difficult to work with her. Now she has a new perspective on the relationship and how they can successfully work together without Athena feeling demeaned. By the way, one of her Life Lessons is Partnership. When she learned that it helped her see the significance of the relationships in her life.

My passion is helping people create their Destiny Roadmap by utilizing the tools in these steps, intuitive coaching, and their Akashic Records. I didn't know this at first; I discovered it by walking away from a six-figure job, landing in The Void once again, and figuring a new approach.

When Marco said, *It's important to make choices based on what is going to fill you and your soul and the money will come,* I decided to own that proudly.

Adding in the layer of the Akashic Records was key for the creation of my Destiny Roadmap, and has brought me the fulfillment I'd always been searching for. When we answer the Soul Calling with trust and confidence, we begin to shift our lives in unimaginable ways. Hopefully we understand by now that when we get out of our heads and into our hearts, we give ourselves the opportunity to create a life that is beyond possibility, a life that's aligned with our soul desires. A life that's connected to our greatest teacher, our higher self, our soul.

What we learn from our past can certainly have a big influence on what we want to create for our future as soon as we have the chance; we often don't give ourselves the chance. Sometimes it takes a monetary investment or time. It might take patience or a little peeling away of the layers. We may need a little help to get there, but by investing in ourselves, we may find this to be the most important step along our Destiny Roadmap.

As we recognize the signs and opportunities presented, we need to be courageous enough to follow the path, even if we have no idea how we will make it happen. If we think that we can't afford it or we don't have enough time, we can question that thought. *Is it true?* Flip the Stone anyway and see where it leads. We may be pleasantly surprised by what we co-create.

Chapter 12
WHAT HAVE WE GOT TO LOSE?

"Everything you want is on the other side of fear."

JACK CANFIELD

What have we got to lose? Truthfully, once we complete the steps, the answer is, a lot. It will happen when we least expect it, in a way that we never could've imagined. Eventually, we will get in our own way, because life begins to feel amazing. I know it sounds cruel, but it's true. We can step in our way and trip ourselves up by getting in our heads and believing what they have to tell us. It will be gloriously painful; it will feel like we slid all the way back to square one. It will stop us in our tracks.

Here's the thing, when we're in it, it feels so unbelievably real, like there's no way out. It's so hard to see it when it's happening, even when we know all about its underhanded ways.

We cover a lot of ground on the journey to discover our Destiny Roadmap. We can't discuss what we'll realize without discussing that it's entirely possible to actually lose much of the ground we'll gain if we're not vigilant about keeping up with the practices and reaching for our toolbox, when needed. We might even need some assistance to help us stay on track.

When clients start co-creating and feeling good, many decide to test the water and see if they're *cured*. It's not what they think they're doing at the time, but it is. I've done this too. During my time in The Void, I stopped meditating for weeks. Soon after I stopped, my mind took over, and I was worrying at a furious pace. I left my heart out of the equation, and I was freaking out about finances and what we weren't doing. I lost my center and my trust in the path I was on. It was incredible how fast it all returned. I didn't just decide to stop meditating to test the theory. My schedule was pretty packed at the time, and I thought I was having difficulties fitting my spiritual practice into my daily life. That is exactly what can easily happen to most of us. The truth was, I didn't make time for it, and I saw the backslide pretty quickly. Once I readjusted, I got back on track, but I saw for myself how easy it is to find ourselves falling into old habits and ways of thinking, even though we've seen the benefits of our hard work in action.

Whether we're new to the concepts in these steps or not, it's entirely possible to find success just by applying ourselves diligently. These tools work, especially in the way they're presented. Clients are putting these concepts into action in their lives and seeing results. We can read this book and go through each step and see growth. It's entirely likely we'll feel better just by adopting a meditation practice. This is what we want, right? Absolutely.

We have everything within us to be successful, and we can do it on our own, but there's a strong chance our mind will butt in at some point and cause fear and uncertainty. If that happens, pick the book back up, and check in again on any step that calls you. Sometimes you can just hold the book and think about your fear(s) and open to a page. Odds are there will be something helpful there. One great tool is the FEAR Method; this is the biggest tool we have to help us along the way.

There are people who will read this book and decide they can't waste any more time; once they've opened up the door into The Void, they know can't go back. They don't want to get to the end of the book and forget why they were drawn to it in the first place. They aren't willing to risk the slide backwards into the pain of where they were, but they won't take immediate action by reaching out. Please know, there is a way to do this where it doesn't have to be so painful. If you're in that place, reach out. Let's talk. This is my passion; I wrote this book for you.

If you're committed to finding your way out of The Void using this guidebook, there are some things you can do to increase your success rate. Within the first weeks of creating their Destiny Roadmap, I ask clients to write down why they started the journey in the first place. I want them to have something to remind them of where they were, what led them to me. When we start feeling better, we can forget how much pain we were in, but it's not that far behind us, and while we don't want to spend a bunch of time looking in the rearview mirror, we do want to make sure we don't forget what got us there. I'd recommend making that list for yourself so you have a reminder handy when you need it.

Please know, we all fall down, and it's important not to be hard on ourselves when it happens. Just be sure to get back up, and don't give up.

Some people do. They get inspired to make lasting changes in their life, and then, after a few weeks, they're right back in their old hurt, grasping for their comfort zone like it's their favorite sweater on a cold day. This is the zone that wasn't serving them in the first place, the one that drove them to pick up this book. Our souls are calling us to find our way out of The Void. There is an incredible life waiting for us in the freedom. Don't turn around unless there's something worth returning to; is it in alignment with your heart or is your head telling you to be practical?

There will be obstacles; we'll continue to have painful experiences. Everything is not going to be happy bunnies eating grass on a sunny day. When the going gets tough, many will get off track. Some will even throw in the towel, because the steps aren't integrated enough in their lives to be the *go-to* aid. Maybe they don't pause long enough to understand the signs and messages that are always there. Some aren't fully committed. They say they want to co-create a new life, but then they freak out and wonder what the hell they're doing when it becomes a little challenging. Fear begins to creep back in. They may push away the growth and fall into resistance, convincing themselves that the negative narrative has something important to say.

In a strange twist, they may actually become complacent in their success along the way and put the tools back in their toolbox, forgetting them completely. We forget how easy it is to get off track, especially when we're feeling good – we can get turned around. In no time, we're back where we were, caught up in our daily dramas, led by our fear. You're probably going to believe your mind when it tells you, *We don't have enough time to do anything on our Soul Care Plan, to practice the steps, to journal or meditate.* It will chime in and pressure you on why you're investing in yourself or trying to figure out what your soul is calling for. You don't have to let it win that argument.

These days, I'm so aware of how uncomfortable it is to be out of alignment with my heart and therefore my truth, to be trapped in my head. I don't want to be there any longer than is necessary. It feels like slow torture: the deep gut sink, the heart palpitations, the feeling that something is stuck in my throat because I'm not speaking up. It's all unbearable anymore, and yet I find myself back there from time to time, feeling like I'm trying to stuff myself into those jeans that are two sizes too small.

That's why I work with a coach. I didn't make real progress until I found a coach who was experienced in what I wanted to achieve, someone who knew how to help me get where I wanted to be. It's why great athletes hire coaches, to get where they want to be. The right coach can accelerate our growth, and, while we're required to face our challenges and do the work, we can move through our experiences more quickly.

We don't want to lose focus in The Void, because it can mean we stay there much longer than is necessary. And we don't want to get comfortable with inaction distraction either. We learn to get comfortable with the unknown, because there's possibility in it, but losing focus is not the same thing. It means we're more susceptible to losing our way and spinning out.

If we can stay on the path of discovering our Destiny Roadmap in The Void, we have the power to co-create an incredible life that feels more aligned with our heart and soul than we could have ever imagined. We have the power to own our freedom when we stay on course and keep moving forward, even when we're afraid.

Chapter 13
CONCLUSION

*"Your time is limited, so don't waste it living someone else's life.
Don't be trapped by dogma – which is living with
the results of other people's thinking.
Don't let the noise of other's opinions drown out your own inner voice.
And most important, have the courage to follow your heart and
intuition. They somehow already know what you truly want
to become. Everything else is secondary."*

STEVE JOBS

February 3, 2016

The first melodic notes of *This Year's Love* by David Gray filtered through the room. As I listened to his soothing voice, tears pooled in my eyes and slowly began to fall down my cheeks. Standing on my yoga mat, I finally understood who I was and what I'd been denying for the last few years, maybe for forever. I was crying and laughing from the realization that, for the first time in my life, I was completely free – not just free from the actual stress of my experience, but free in my heart, mind, and soul. As I looked over the jungle outside the window of my rental, I knew I was ready to step up and be who I came here to be. It was time to show up for my life and enjoy all of it, without fear, no matter where it led me.

I wrote this in my journal:

> *Today I cried from the sheer joy of my life and freedom from the people and things that have weighed me down. I am open in my heart and alive in my soul. The expansiveness I feel is entirely enveloped around my body and my heart. It's filling me with pure joy and pure light. I am clear and understand that choosing what I want is healing, liberating, and freeing.*
>
> *Knowing when I chose to walk away, to no longer stay in the negativity and pain, was an experience that required trust and courage. I chose the easier, lighter way because I can. I am worthy of a life that fills me with joy, peace, abundance, happiness, sunshine, heart-expanding love, and grounding. I will not hide who I am.*

For most of my adult life, I've listened to my heart, and I felt like I'd been doing the personal soul work by staying dedicated, always, to my spiritual growth, no matter how hard it was. What I now know is that I wasn't completely free. I was trapped in my mind at times, even though I knew better.

I did everything right. I went to energy practitioners; I ended relationships that weren't healthy; I followed where I was led. I grew and lived on the edge of my comfort zone with dedication, but I wasn't free.

Because I'd been in The Void a number of times before this most recent trip through, I knew there had to be a way to do it differently, because I wasn't truly, all-encompassingly happy. I mean joyous, blissful, deep peace, worry-free, centered, enlightened happiness: the kind of happiness that comes with freedom, the freedom to be yourself completely. I wasn't living my truth. I was living for who I thought I should be as I moved through life. I was always searching for something else, thinking alcohol, men, drugs, a new car, my own home, marriage, or a job title would fill the gaping hole. They never did unconditionally.

I had been in so much pain before I walked into the rooms of AA more than 20 years ago, I never wanted to go back there again. In that program, I saw the way out was to work on myself and be of service to others. Everything opened up for me at that time, and I held onto that, *always*.

It didn't mean I did everything perfectly, but I sure tried. I've dragged around this idea that I had to do things the right way. I wore it like a permanent facial tattoo I got one night in a black-out in Mexico. *A little too much tequila!* I don't have any tattoos, but that's what it felt like. Every time I'd look at myself in the mirror or feel into who I was, I'd see that invisible tattoo and what it represented. I rarely saw past the exterior into the interior, the beauty of my soul.

I wasn't completely satisfied, which drove me further down my spiritual path. So it's not a bad thing, but at some point I had to stop and ask myself, *What am I trying to achieve?* I was clearly still trying to escape, because I was afraid to let people in fully. Since you're still reading, I'm pretty sure this is probably your story too.

We're afraid to reveal who we are, completely. Unsure how to show up for ourselves with love and compassion. We may show up in the fact that we just keep moving forward, no matter what, but we're chasing something. My friend and mentor, Peggy, supported and pushed me to be who I came here to be, but I was afraid to go deeply inside and find my truth. I allowed myself to play small. This was no way to live. When we play small, we deny ourselves the experience of living the life we're meant to live. We tamp down our fire in the name of not burning someone else. We keep our light dim, because we're concerned we might be seen.

We can dip our toe in the water, but never really dive in completely, and that's a painful place to be. Showing up for ourselves is one of the hardest things to do. Being in service to ourselves is uncomfortable, so we cling to the raft as our only life support.

Remember those landmines I saw around me when I was trying to figure out how to step into my power? Along the way, I realized they were really stepping stones to my inner strength. Some of them were painful experiences, and some of them were amazing. All of them were helping me find the courage to be who I'm meant be in this lifetime and share that with others. They were my Life Lessons made manifest.

We can feel happy for so much of our journey, because we're smart and we apply ourselves, but it can waver, because the mind is strong in its convictions. What we find through the process of co-creating the Destiny Roadmap is the importance of release, patience, and heart-opening freedom. I didn't have the additional layer of freedom within my happiness until I created my Destiny Roadmap and gained the understanding of why I felt connected and fulfilled by certain people, jobs, places, and experiences in my life.

When I went ahead and made my way up the side of that pyramid in Tulum, even though I was scared to death, I told my fear I was taking over the driver's seat from now on. When I arrived at the top, and the shell around my heart obliterated. It was like a butterfly emerged from its chrysalis. I was free. In those moments, we're released from the traps we set for ourselves, the ones that we use every day for protection, the ones we utilize in order to make sure we don't feel too much or get too close, so we don't get hurt. Typically, we're hiding in some way, and we don't notice until we do something out of the ordinary, something courageous that would normally have us sitting on the sidelines. We arrive at the top of a pyramid and find our new self waiting there. I was afraid to be in my power, which is why I couldn't step into it. I was afraid the other shoe was going to drop, so I never put them fully on.

When we look back on the experience that brought us into The Void, we can see the protections we created did nothing to keep us from being hurt. We understand that every one of our fears rose up to knock us down, so what good were our protections except to confine us to live at the whims of our fear and worry? By walking away, we find the courage to answer back to our fear. We answer the Soul Calling, and we begin to work on forming the right questions and receiving the answers.

When we co-create our Destiny Roadmap, we can melt the shell around our heart and link up with who we're meant to be in this lifetime. Not who we were, because that person is typically gone as we make the decision to go forward. We leave her when we make the choice to walk fully into The Void and close the door behind us. We say goodbye to her when we say hello to the journey of the unknown. When I participated fully in the magic of Tulum, I was becoming the person who would walk out the other side of The Void. At some point, I stopped walking away and began walking toward my new self, the one I was finding through the steps and the experiences.

Here's what I know for sure. When it's our time nothing can stop us, but if we don't take action nothing can start us either. We can deal with the fear, but what hangs on the longest is the ability to get marooned in our heads. At some point, we can give ourselves permission to be truly free and enjoy our lives in every moment, and in every corner and crevice.

It's about having an open heart and welcoming the adventure. It's about living in the moment and creating the life we know, so deep in our heart, that we were meant to live. It's about facing our fears with courage and sometimes humor. It's about listening to our heart and soul and going on the journey, even though we have no idea where it will take us, but we know for a fact it will be better than we could've ever imagined. It's knowing we can enjoy every moment completely, that we can be deeply happy and we don't have to wait for the other shoe to drop. We can enjoy it for as long as it lasts, because what I've found is, it lasts as long as we choose.

What brings us into The Void, that first door, is the door to freedom. The Soul Calling is waking us up to our potential release and opportunities. The Void is really about life and the tools are applied every day in the name of freeing our soul, because we have the option to go *big* when we find ourselves in the place where one door has closed and another has yet to open.

On my first day in Tulum, a family of Toucans appeared outside my bedroom window. We watched each other for 20 minutes, and I posted it on my Facebook page. A year later, I was reminded of the experience by a Facebook memory and it occurred to me that I had never looked up Toucan totem medicine. It read, in part, *to show you that you can safely take off your mask and reveal the truth of your inner self.*

Perfection! I didn't look it up when it happened, but the message was so important, it found a way to get it back to me again.

Thank you for going on this journey with me. I hope you find the freedom to co-create and follow your own Destiny Roadmap, because it's our birthright to live full out in alignment with our soul. When we embrace The Void, we allow our soul and our light to shine brightly, and that light is needed in this world, now more than ever.

We have everything inside us to live the life of our dreams, even if we don't know what our dreams are, yet. It's always there, it just requires courage to open the door to discover it. Isn't it time to fully enjoy the ride?

"The divide between where you are and where you're meant to be is not as wide as your mind tells you it is."

Kelli Reese

SUGGESTED READING

Exploratory Surgery for the Soul, by Dr. Peggy Farmer

Creative Visualization, by Shakti Gawain

The Way of the Peaceful Warrior, by Dan Millman

Illusions, The Adventures of a Reluctant Messiah, by Richard Bach

Edgar Cayce on the Akashic Records, by Kevin J. Todeschi

You Can Heal Your Life, by Louise Hay

The Fire Starter Sessions, by Danielle LaPorte

Many Lives, Many Masters, by Dr. Brian Weiss

How to Coach Difficult People, by Kris Plachy

Change Your Think, by Kris Plachy

The Difference – 10 Steps to Writing a Book That Matters, by Dr. Angela Lauria

ACKNOWLEDGMENTS

This book came together with the help of many along my path. There are always invaluable people behind the scenes who really are the shining stars, and back stage in my world is no exception. This book would not have been written without the following three ladies: my book developer Angela Lauria at Difference Press, my life coach, mentor and dear friend, Peggy Farmer, and Kris Plachy, leadership coach extraordinaire.

Angela, thank you for helping me finally write a book. I don't know how many more years I would have sat around "trying to write a book that could make a difference." Your program made a huge difference in my life. I'm forever grateful.

Peggy, your unending support and love have seen me through it all. Your strength and guidance have been so important. My emergency brake is off! I love you and Hector.

Kris, I don't know what I would have done without your wisdom and poignant questions. . Thank you for your expertise.

To the very first clients who trusted me and signed up for the Destiny Roadmap program before it was even fully created, your commitment and insight made it possible for me to create a program that continues to help so many more. Thank you.

To the first clients who gave me the honor of reading their Akashic Records. You helped me discover the opportunity to combine my love of coaching with my desire to help people with my intuitive abilities. I'm forever grateful.

Maggie McReynolds, I've only experienced one Managing Editor so far, but the next one has some big shoes to fill. Thank you for your encouragement, honesty, and patience.

To the Morgan James Publishing team: Special thanks to David Hancock, CEO & Founder for believing in me and my message. To my Author Relations Manager, Aubrey Kosa, thanks for making the process seamless and easy. Many more thanks to everyone else, but especially Jim Howard, Bethany Marshall, and Nickcole Watkins.

My sister, Pam, without you, it would definitely not be as much fun. Thanks for being on the journey and for always supporting me and my dreams. Love you, Scott, Chris, and Michael.

Joe Duckett, you've always believed in my ability to do anything. There aren't many husbands who would move three times and start their business over each time for their wife's career. You are truly amazing and an awesome example of trust in the ability to co-create anything. You are truly my best friend.

Sarah Griffith, thank you for your mad woo-woo skills and your chiropractic excellence. You pulled me through a number of times. Bless you.

Karen, meeting you more than 20 years ago was a gift I will never take for granted. I would not have made it through those early years without you. I love you!

Liza Tedesco and Lucinda Berdon, best Tulum traveling mates ever! So much love for you ladies.

Lisa Landry and Anna Ward. I am forever grateful for the opportunity to work with both of you. Your friendship and support means everything to me!

There are many people who've positively impacted my life in many ways. I couldn't mention all of you here, but please know that you are in my heart.

Finally, to you for taking the time to read this book and perhaps even apply the steps to co-create a life you love.

ABOUT THE AUTHOR

Kelli Reese is an International Bestselling Author and Intuitive Coach. She works with Soulful Entrepreneurs and helps them identify their blocks and grow the business they know they're capable of.

In her work, Kelli bridges spirituality with business and utilizes more than a decade of self-mastery work, a 17 year career in management and the experience of building two personal businesses from the ground up. Her certifications in yoga, polarity therapy, leadership coaching and the Akashic Records are the foundation of her work.

In 2015, Kelli walked away from a six-figure job running a $34mm organization. She applied her skill set to her own life and peeled away the layers to reconnect with her soul and where it was guiding her. The Destiny Roadmap is the culmination of that exploration and the exact steps she took to create a business and life she loves.

Kelli lives in Tulum, MX. After the life changing trip to Tulum she writes about in *The Destiny Roadmap*, she knew Tulum was meant to be her home. It's where she's most aligned, centered and able to do her best work. Kelli offers regular workshops in Mexico for her clients to experience the magic of Tulum and work directly with her in the transformational place she loves.

THANK YOU

Thanks for reading!

If you've come this far, I'm so grateful. I know there are tools in this book you can immediately utilize in your life. If you'd like some clarity or you're not sure where to start, I'd love to hear from you; especially if you're staring into the abyss of The Void and wondering what, if anything, is on the other side. Feel free to drop me an email at kelli@kellireese.com.

In addition, as a THANK YOU, I've created a 4 step plan to Find Your Freedom. Hop over to https://www.kellireese.com/thedestinyroadmap to sign up. It's a daily approach to get connected and start moving forward in your life.

Morgan James
Speakers Group

We connect Morgan James published
authors with live and online events
and audiences who will benefit
from their expertise.

CPSIA information can be obtained
at www.ICGtesting.com
Printed in the USA
BVHW04s1537180518
516658BV00001B/200/P

9 781683 507291